BRITAIN'S BEST POLITICAL CARTOONS 2025

Dr Tim Benson is Britain's leading authority on political cartoons. He runs the Political Cartoon Gallery and Café which is located near the River Thames in Putney. He has produced numerous books on the history of cartoons, including *David Low Censored*, *Giles's War*, *Low and the Dictators*, *The Cartoon Century: Modern Britain through the Eyes of Its Cartoonists*, *Drawing the Curtain: The Cold War in Cartoons*, *Over the Top: A Cartoon History of Australia at War*, *How to be British: A Cartoon Celebration*, *Churchill: A Life in Cartoons*, *Drawn to the Promised Land: A Cartoon History of Britain, Palestine and the Jews: 1917–1949* and *The Second World War in Cartoons*.

BRITAIN'S BEST POLITICAL CARTOONS 2025

Edited by Tim Benson

Hutchinson Heinemann

UK | USA | Canada | Ireland | Australia
India | New Zealand | South Africa

Hutchinson Heinemann is part of the Penguin Random House group of companies whose addresses can be found at global.penguinrandomhouse.com

Penguin Random House UK,
One Embassy Gardens, 8 Viaduct Gardens, London SW11 7BW

penguin.co.uk
global.penguinrandomhouse.com

First published 2025
001

Cartoons copyright © contributing cartoonists, 2025
Essay, captions and selection copyright © Tim Benson, 2025

The moral right of the author has been asserted

Penguin Random House values and supports copyright. Copyright fuels creativity, encourages diverse voices, promotes freedom of expression and supports a vibrant culture. Thank you for purchasing an authorised edition of this book and for respecting intellectual property laws by not reproducing, scanning or distributing any part of it by any means without permission. You are supporting authors and enabling Penguin Random House to continue to publish books for everyone. No part of this book may be used or reproduced in any manner for the purpose of training artificial intelligence technologies or systems. In accordance with Article 4(3) of the DSM Directive 2019/790, Penguin Random House expressly reserves this work from the text and data mining exception.

Typeset in 11/15.5pt Amasis MT Light by Six Red Marbles UK, Thetford, Norfolk

Printed and bound in Italy by L.E.G.O. S.p.A.

The authorised representative in the EEA is Penguin Random House Ireland, Morrison Chambers, 32 Nassau Street, Dublin D02 YH68

A CIP catalogue record for this book is available from the British Library

ISBN: 978–1–529–15527–3

Penguin Random House is committed to a sustainable future for our business, our readers and our planet. This book is made from Forest Stewardship Council® certified paper.

INTRODUCTION

A cartoon shows a naked politician eating a baby. The caption reads: 'What's wrong ... you never seen a politician kissing babies before?' A second cartoon depicts a leader constructing a wall. It's formed from human limbs and blood.

Dave Brown, *Independent*, 27 January 2003

Political cartoons often set out to shock. These two, however, caused not only shock but controversy when they first appeared. Dave Brown's 2003 rendering of a naked Ariel Sharon – then prime minister of Israel – eating a bloodied Palestinian baby might, in the artist's eyes, have been a reference to Goya's painting *Saturn Devouring One of His Sons*, but to the Israeli Embassy in London it was antisemitic – a visual evocation of the age-old 'blood libel' that falsely held that Jews used human blood in their religious rituals. The image 'would not have looked out of place in *Der Stürmer*', an embassy spokesman said. Gerald Scarfe's 2013 cartoon for the *Sunday Times* – produced in response to Prime Minister Benjamin Netanyahu's championing of the physical wall between Israelis and Palestinians – was similarly met by a storm of criticism, and for the same reason: Scarfe's cartoon, his critics argued, perpetuated the blood libel trope.

Brown's editor, Simon Kelner, defended his cartoonist's work: 'I'm a Jew myself, so I will be sensitive to anything antisemitic,' he said to the *Jewish Chronicle*. 'The cartoon was very powerful, but it was against Sharon and not the Jewish people.' Gerald Scarfe's employers, by contrast, refused to back him. The acting editor of the *Sunday Times*,

Gerald Scarfe, *Sunday Times*, 27 January 2013

Martin Ivens, apologised unreservedly to Jewish community leaders for what he said was 'a terrible mistake'. Scarfe's work was renowned for being 'consistently brutal and bloody', but here the artist had 'crossed a line'. The paper's owner, Rupert Murdoch, stated unequivocally on Twitter: 'Gerald Scarfe has never reflected the opinions of the *Sunday Times*. Nevertheless, we owe a major apology for this grotesque, offensive cartoon.'

Scrutiny and criticism of cartoons that address the long-running conflict between Israelis and Palestinians have, if anything, become even more intense over the past two years, in the wake of the 7 October 2023 attacks by Hamas on Israeli civilians and the subsequent military campaign initiated by the Israeli government. So angry and polarised are views, indeed, that cartoonists who engage in visual commentary on 7 October and its aftermath regularly run the risk of charges of antisemitism, Islamophobia, or more generalised racism.

The furore surrounding a cartoon by the *Guardian*'s former cartoonist Steve Bell, produced in the immediate aftermath of the events of 7 October, is a case in point. Bell's cartoon was a response to the retaliatory 'surgical strike' on the Gaza Strip that Benjamin Netanyahu promised by way of response to the Hamas attacks. Sceptical as to whether such a precise operation was practically possible, Bell elected to depict the Israeli prime minister cutting a Gaza Strip-shaped outline on his own stomach with a scalpel while wearing boxing gloves. His inspiration, he said, was a cartoon produced in 1966 by David Levine that showed US President Lyndon B. Johnson bearing a Vietnam-shaped scar on his torso (the words 'After David Levine' appear towards the bottom of Bell's cartoon). Colleagues at the *Guardian*, however,

Steve Bell, *Guardian*, 10 October 2023

worried that the cartoon might be accused of antisemitism: the image of an Israeli politician cutting into his own stomach, they suggested, might well evoke, for some, the Jewish money lender Shylock in Shakespeare's *Merchant of Venice* and his demand for a 'pound of flesh'. Bell was emphatic that it was the Levine cartoon, not an antisemitic trope, that he was seeking to evoke. 'I don't promote harmful antisemitic stereotypes,' he said, adding that Shylock had 'nothing to do' with his creation. The *Guardian* took a different view and refused to run the cartoon. Steve Bell responded by posting the cartoon on X, where it went viral. The *Guardian* then fired him.

Bell later admitted that he knew that 'the *Guardian* don't like having their editorial processes discussed in the open', and that by going public with

David Levine, *New York Review of Books*, 1966

the cartoon he was 'asking for trouble'. It was a very sad end to a working relationship that stretched back forty years, and, for Peter Brookes at *The Times*, 'a very sad day for political cartooning'. Steve Bell, he told *Press Gazette*, 'has been hugely influential over the years, and I think his ability to puncture the overblown egos of the political class has been second to none'. As for the offending cartoon: 'I don't see it as antisemitic. Anti-Netanyahu, yes, and against his current and proposed policy in Gaza, which threatens the whole population and not just Hamas, the declared (and in my view obviously legitimate) target. Everyone is piling in on that point now, even Biden and Blinken. Steve Bell got there first, and in a febrile atmosphere has paid the price.'

American cartoonist Michael Ramirez, meanwhile, was accused of racism and Islamophobia when he drew a cartoon for the *Washington Post* that showed senior Hamas official Ghazi Hamad using women and children as human shields. 'The caricatures employ racial stereotypes that were offensive and disturbing,' one reader from Fairfax, Virginia, wrote. 'Depicting Arabs with exaggerated features and portraying women in derogatory, stereotypical roles perpetuates racism and gender bias, which is wholly unacceptable.' For her part, Suzanne van Geuns, a research associate at Princeton University, argued that as 'a scholar of religion and media' she recognised 'a deeply racist depiction of the "heathen" and his barbarous cruelty toward women and children', adding: 'It is in no way informative, helpful or thought-provoking to look at this conflict through the glasses of 19th-century colonialists.' On X, the British journalist Owen Jones concurred: 'It's not even subtle in its racism. This racist dehumanisation is always a precondition for mass murder of the sort currently taking place in Gaza.' The *Washington Post*'s section editor, David Shipley, issued an apology: 'The reaction to the image convinced me that I had missed something profound, and divisive, and I regret that.'

Ramirez expressed himself dumbfounded by the criticism. His cartoon was not aimed at the Palestinians in general, he said, but at Hamas and at Ghazi Hamad – Hamad had, after all, hailed the 7 October attack and pledged that it would be repeated again and again until Israel was 'removed'. 'This cartoon was designed with specificity,' Ramirez said in a piece for *Newsweek*. 'Its focus is on a specific individual and the statements he made on behalf of a specific organisation he represents – their claims of victimhood, and the plight of innocent Palestinians used as pawns in their political and military strategy. That person is Ghazi Hamad . . . The organisation is Hamas. The main figure in the cartoon is labeled Hamas . . . Gaza civilians are victims. Hamas is not . . . Critics of my cartoon are using an accusation of racism as a device to "cancel" the

Michael Ramirez, *Washington Post*, 9 November 2023

truth – the overwhelming empirical evidence that Hamas uses civilians, both Palestinians and Israelis, as human shields.' He was sharply critical of the *Washington Post*'s decision to remove the cartoon from its website: 'Journalists have an obligation to keep the lights on and not kowtow to the voices of dissent who want to extinguish the free exchange of ideas and hide in the darkness. From my perspective, I think it hurt the *Washington Post* far more than me.'

Such angrily debated incidents show how easy it is to be misconstrued – or lay oneself open to being misconstrued – when passions run high. Time and time again cartoonists have said they are seeking to get one message across while being accused of relaying a very different one. Ramirez claimed to be criticising an individual. His detractors said he was lambasting an entire people. Cartoonists who have set out to castigate Benjamin Netanyahu have been taken to task by those who interpret their work as anti-Zionist or antisemitic. Nick Newman, the pocket cartoonist for the *Sunday Times*, relates how 'even before October 7 I was wary of covering the conflict – partly because editors didn't want to go there for fear of causing outrage and partly because, as a pocket cartoonist, I try to be funny rather than chin-stroking, and there has not been much to be funny about before or after October 7.'

Nick Newman, *The Sunday Times*, 9 February 2025

He goes on: 'The Israeli reaction to cartoons critical of the Israeli Government has led to cartoonists being cancelled and sacked. Almost any criticism is labelled as antisemitism – and editors and cartoonists just don't want the fight. In that respect, the censors have won.'

Peter Schrank expresses a similar view:

> 'It's easy to upset and offend people with a Jewish background who have much emotion and hope invested in the idea of the Jewish State as the final and ultimate refuge (this was beautifully portrayed in the recent film *The Brutalist*). They can be strongly offended if Israel is criticised, leading to a very emotional response. Unfortunately, this is devaluing the very serious charge of antisemitism. Israeli politicians and officials are too often too quick to use this accusation when faced with criticism.'

For his part Peter Brookes is simultaneously sharply critical of Hamas's actions and rhetoric against Israel, and of the military action in the Gaza Strip authorised by Israel's leader: 'You cannot ignore the horrendous figures of deaths of women and children.' As a result, he says, 'you find yourself condemning the bombing in Gaza whilst your heart goes out to those Israeli families whose family members are still being held hostage.' That is not a message destined to be well received by the more partisan on either side of the divide. In the words of former *Private Eye* cartoonist Zoom Rockman: 'In many ways it's a tribal conflict. Morality exists within the group and hostility is external. So any expressions of what's right and wrong to all people is going to offend someone.' Or, as Andy Davey puts it: 'One of the great things about good editorial cartoons is that they contain a certain ambiguity; a problematic quality in the "heat-oppressed brain" of the single-minded. Lurking in the shade are the perceived beasts and bêtes noires of antisemitism and Islamophobia, ready to pounce in an instant.'

Peter Brookes, *The Times*, 26 July 2025

* * *

How, then, do newspapers and cartoonists set about negotiating such difficult and contentious terrain? The answer, in many cases, is that they seek to avoid it altogether. Editors at the *Telegraph*, according to Patrick Blower, generally discourage cartoons on the conflict because they regard them as potentially too 'incendiary'. Blower's colleague, Andy Davey, agrees. Editors, he says, 'want to ignore the whole thing. Their motives are almost certainly not pure, but I can see that avoiding the issue is the easiest path.' It's a similar state of affairs at *The Times*, Peter Schrank suggests. 'Whether through pressure from editors or self-censorship, we've all been guilty of keeping to the safety of domestic politics, or hitting the huge and easy target of Trump, while ignoring the horrors in the Middle East . . . I think they [the editors] just don't want to go there for cartoons.' He recalls an occasion when he submitted a couple of Gaza-related cartoons – 'neither of them being particularly tough' – but had both rejected.

An alternative response has been to try to come up with cartoons that are even-handed. On the day after the 7 October attacks, for example, the *Guardian* ran a cartoon that showed two children, one Israeli, one Palestinian, cowering under tables while rockets were being fired over both their heads. 'There have been heavy civilian casualties on both sides after a weekend of fighting' the accompanying description ran. Two days later the words 'Violence continues to escalate in Israel and Gaza' were accompanied by an illustration of a forlorn planet Earth descending an escalator towards a dystopian

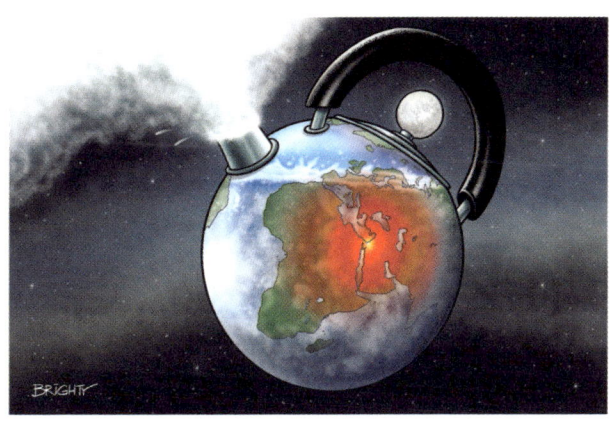

Steve Bright, *Sun*, 23 October 2023

hell. Over at the *Sun*, Steve Bright says that he has 'only done one cartoon [showing the world close to boiling point] on the current conflict which did not seek to apportion blame more to one side than another, far less take sides'.

Some might argue that there can be no such thing as even-handedness in such a long-running and blood-soaked conflict, where perspectives are not only shaped by the apparent rights and wrongs of the actions of the day under review, but also by all that has gone before (as Zoom Rockman puts it: 'Every time you think you've heard the story of who started it first, someone points out something that happened previously and before you know it you're all the way back to Moses (who was Jewish by the way).') Steve Bright's plea for 'objectivity' and avoiding 'the risk of being sucked into the rhetoric of one side over the other' is praiseworthy. His view that 'our cartoons need to be about war versus peace, not Israel versus Palestine', however, is not an easy one to sustain in practice.

It's instructive in this context to consider the *Private Eye* front cover of the 20 October–2 November 2023 issue. Rather than run the usual photograph with caption or speech bubbles, the paper opted for a stark block of text that read: 'Warning: This magazine may contain some criticism of the Israeli government and may suggest that killing everyone in Gaza as revenge for Hamas atrocities may not be a good long-term solution to the problems of the region.' For some, such a sentiment comes across as balanced. For Zoom Rockman, however – then working for *Private Eye* – the wording was dangerously emotive. 'I was quite disappointed with the cover itself,' he said. 'I wrote a letter to them [*Private Eye*] after I saw that cover, saying that just because they made the distinction between the Israeli government and Jewish people, doesn't mean that ignorant people won't. Because every time this conflict flares up, just random Jewish people are targeted, and we're seeing it more and more. But what's worse is they exaggerated the Israeli position. They framed it as Israel wanting, and having an active policy, to kill everyone in Gaza. And because it was so incendiary, I really had a problem with it, because I felt it would lead to more antisemitic attacks.'

Rockman's disappointment with *Private Eye* was not a one-off. After a cartoon he had drawn mocking antisemitism in the UK had appeared in the paper, he received an anonymous message on X that read: 'Hope both you and your extended family get to meet Hamas in person, very soon.' X declined to take down the post saying it did not breach its safety policies, but it was later removed from the platform after Rockman contacted the Community Security Trust, a charity focused on protecting the British Jewish community. Rockman subsequently wrote to *Private Eye*'s letters page about the threat, but did not receive a reply. He later said: 'I think after *Charlie Hebdo* [the French satirical magazine that has been the target of several terrorist attacks],

Zoom Rockman, October 2023

Zoom Rockman, *Private Eye*, October 2023

and stuff like this, they should care about their cartoonists and whether they have received death threats. I was waiting for a response from them, and I haven't had one.' In the end, 'disappointed and disrespected', he decided to resign.

* * *

The best political cartoons have always upset one individual or another, or one group or another. After all, that's what they're there to do. Whether it's the future George IV furious at Gillray's depictions of him as a decadent spendthrift, or the Conservative government of the late 1930s angered by David Low's mockery of its policy of appeasement, the satirical barbs of the greatest cartoonists have hit their mark and infuriated or wounded their target as they did so. But the complexities of the conflict between Israelis and Palestinians, the immense suffering it has caused, and the intense emotions that it has given rise to, have rendered it a fiendishly difficult territory for contemporary cartoonists to negotiate.

Should they even attempt to do so? Andy Davey, for one, feels that the conflict is best avoided by cartoonists: ' . . . aside from the unpleasant sight of a cosseted, pompous fool with a scratchy pen addressing the deep black gravity of the subject, there are also practical reasons to avoid it – the results tend to be hand-wringing "why-oh-why" images that say nothing, or drawings that cause anger and hatred, however unintentional.' But for every Andy Davey there is a Steve Bell who remains adamant that cartoonists should express their take on events in the region, or a Peter Brookes who argues that it is 'pathetic' not to express one's own opinion and that 'to think it's just too much bother is plain and simple cowardice', or a Peter Schrank who holds that 'it is our job to show concern for the dispossessed, for the vulnerable and exposed.'

I must confess that I'm with those who venture to stick their head above the parapet.

THE CARTOONS

1 September 2024
Morten Morland
Sunday Times

Conservative critics were quick to condemn Sir Keir Starmer's decision to relocate a portrait of Margaret Thatcher from his study to another part of 10 Downing Street. Perhaps surprisingly, the picture had been commissioned by a Labour predecessor, Gordon Brown, in 2007. Starmer told the BBC's Laura Kuenssberg that it was nothing personal but he was fed up with 'images and pictures of people staring down at me', preferring, he suggested, landscapes. Edvard Munch's famously angst-ridden *Scream* (1893) joins other artworks that, in the cartoonist's imagining, seem to suit a mood of 'doom and gloom'.

Seven years after the Grenfell Tower fire claimed the lives of 72 people, a public inquiry published its seven-volume report. It identified 'systematic dishonesty' on the part of cladding and construction companies for installing flammable materials. The report also highlighted the companies' exploitation of lax regulation and the 'decades of failure' by governments to strengthen safeguards, despite warnings about a potential disaster. In 2014, Prime Minister David Cameron had celebrated the ending of 'needless health and safety inspections'. Three years later, and out of office, Lord Cameron installed a shepherd's hut in his garden in which to write his memoirs.

8 September 2024
Chris Riddell
Observer

10 September 2024
Ben Jennings
Guardian

Sir Keir Starmer came to power in July 2024, promising to 'deliver change'. One thing set to change was the winter fuel payment, which, since 1997, had been a universal lump sum paid by the state to millions of UK pensioners. Blaming a 'black hole' in government finances left by the Conservatives, Chancellor Rachel Reeves revealed in late July that she was planning to limit it to the poorest pensioners – those claiming pension credit. Despite a barrage of criticism that many low-income pensioners would be disadvantaged, on 10 September the government defeated a Conservative motion trying to block the measure.

On 10 September 2024, Sir Keir Starmer became the first Labour prime minister in 15 years to address the Trades Union Congress (TUC) annual conference. Union leaders had welcomed the government's quick decisions to accept pay recommendations, thereby resolving disputes with teachers, National Health Service (NHS) workers and train drivers. There were also warm words for plans to improve workers' rights. But the TUC opposed the abandoning of a universal winter fuel payment and any return to 'austerity'. Opposition critics portrayed the Labour leader as being in the pocket of the unions, while Starmer warned unions of 'tough decisions on the horizon'.

10 September 2024
Patrick Blower
Daily Telegraph

During a US presidential election debate, Republican candidate Donald Trump repeated claims that Haitian immigrants in Springfield, Ohio were eating the pets of other residents. Afterwards, the singer–songwriter Taylor Swift endorsed Democratic contender Kamala Harris on Instagram, signing herself 'Childless Cat Lady': a swipe at controversial comments by Trump's running mate, JD Vance. The cartoonist observed: 'This illustrates perfectly why Trump presents such a challenge for satirists. He made his ridiculous statement about immigrants eating pets when I was working on this cartoon and I couldn't believe my luck. We fell over ourselves laughing, but did it hurt him? Not a bit . . . he somehow emerged stronger.'

12 September 2024
Peter Schrank
Economist

In a speech to the King's Fund, a charity devoted to improving healthcare, Sir Keir Starmer announced a decade-long strategy to fix the NHS. There was a catch: 'no more money without reform'. The main strands were more digital technology, more care in the community, and more emphasis on disease prevention. The cartoonist was unimpressed: 'Keir Starmer announced that he and Health Secretary Wes Streeting had a plan for the NHS. My point was that they're never going to get the NHS back on its feet. I was just being cynical, really, which is a pleasure I occasionally allow myself.'

13 September 2024
Peter Brookes
The Times

Two days after his TV debate with Kamala Harris, with its lurid cat-eating discussion, Donald Trump ended speculation about a final bout between the presidential candidates. He declared on his Truth Social platform: 'NO THIRD DEBATE'. Emerging polls suggested that Harris had bested him at their encounter. She thought that 'we owe it to the voters to have another debate'. But Trump insisted that it was only losers who wanted a rematch, and he reiterated his criticism of the ABC network's moderators during what turned out to be their one and only encounter.

14 September 2024
Ben Jennings
i

Under pressure from Russian missile and drone attacks, Ukrainian President Volodymyr Zelensky continued to lobby his allies, particularly the UK and United States, for permission to fire Western-supplied long-range missiles into Russia. Only with this capability, he claimed, could Ukraine strike at the airbases from which the Russian attacks were launched. On 13 September 2024, Sir Keir Starmer and President Joe Biden conferred but came to no decision, leaving Zelensky still, as he put it, 'waiting for the relevant discussions'.

16 September 2024
Rob Murray
Daily Telegraph

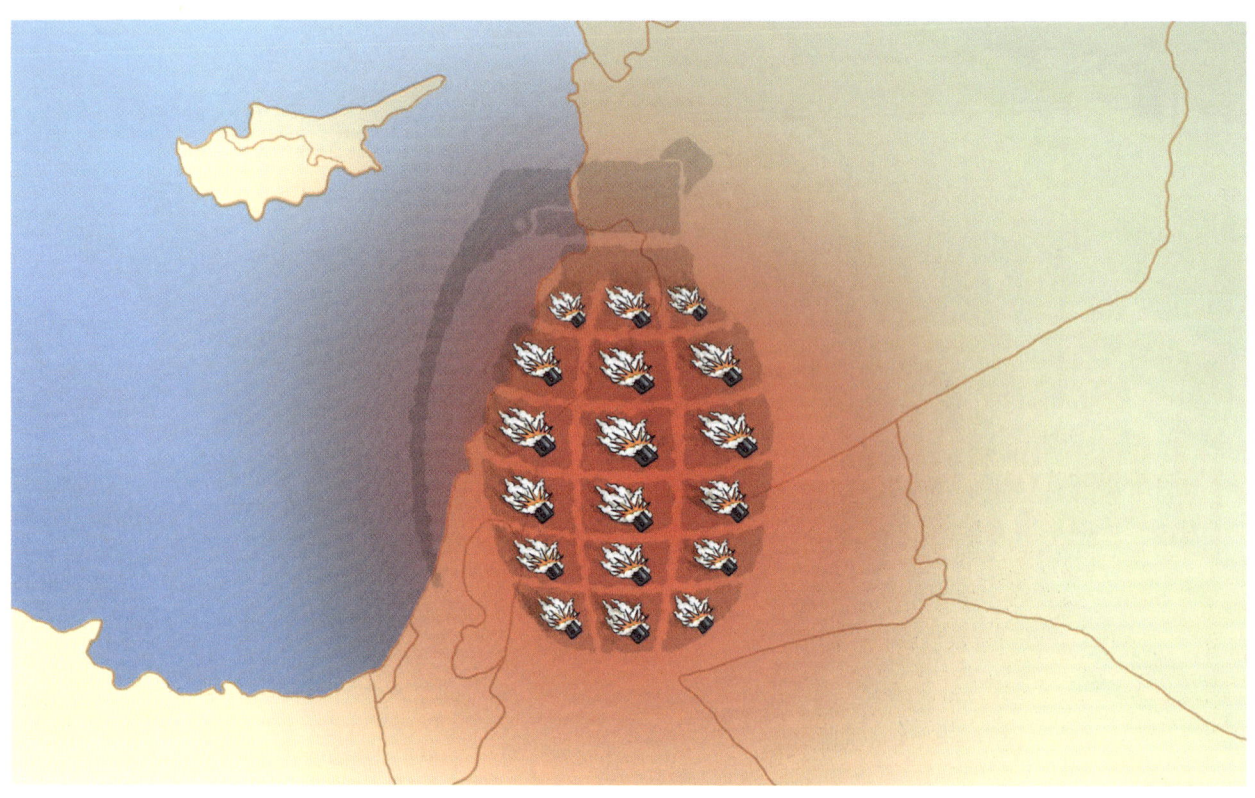

18 September 2024
Nicola Jennings
Guardian

In Lebanon and Syria on 17 September 2024, pagers used by members of the vehemently anti-Israel group, Hezbollah, simultaneously exploded, killing around 20 people and injuring hundreds more. Some news outlets suggested that a message appearing on all the devices, purportedly from Hezbollah leader Hassan Nasrallah, had triggered the remote attack. The next day, walkie-talkies used by Hezbollah and others blew up, in a similar act of sabotage. The group had recently switched away from mobile phones to such lower-tech devices to try and enhance its security. All eyes were on Israel as having infiltrated Hezbollah's supply lines to plant and detonate the gadgets.

As the Liberal Democrats gathered in Brighton, the BBC's political editor, Chris Mason, commented: 'I don't think I've ever seen such undiluted joy at a party conference.' The general election in July 2024 had increased their overall vote share by less than 1 per cent, but a ruthless targeting strategy had boosted their number of seats to 72, an increase of 550 per cent on the previous general-election result. As the cartoonist summarised it: 'Ed Davey had a fun conference and unveiled his Lib Dem frontbench team, which promised to offer a positive alternative to Labour's "doom and gloom".'

19 September 2024
Andy Davey
Daily Telegraph

20 September 2024
Peter Brookes
The Times

Parliament's Register of Members' Financial Interests (2 September 2024) revealed an extensive list of items given to the prime minister, from clothes to accommodation to tickets for the 'Jingle Bell Ball'. 'There was a backlash over Keir Starmer accepting £100,000 in gifts, including multiple pairs of glasses worth £2,485,' observed the cartoonist, adding: 'He doesn't have much of a political instinct, as shown by this whole freebie thing. I really don't think he could see what was right there in front of him until he was so up against it that he had to apologise and give back some of the money.'

Notable among the gifts registered by the prime minister were tickets and pre-match hospitality at various football grounds across the UK. On the heels of this came a claim that Starmer, an Arsenal fan and season-ticket holder, had been granted the use of a corporate box at the club's Emirates Stadium after becoming prime minister. According to Reuters Fact Check, Arsenal denied it but acknowledged that Sir Keir had been offered seats in the directors' box 'on occasion', while Starmer said that the new arrangements were a reluctant concession to security. Labour's 2024 party conference opened on 22 September.

20 September 2024
Ben Jennings
Guardian

25 September 2024
Steven Camley
Glasgow Herald

Sir Keir Starmer delivered his party leader's speech on 24 September, the closing day of Labour's annual conference. Although it was mostly devoted to Labour's domestic achievements and challenges, he called 'again for an immediate ceasefire in Gaza' and, more bafflingly, for 'the return of the sausages'. He had meant to say 'hostages' and immediately corrected himself; but inevitably the gaffe took on a life of its own on social media. Labour donor Waheed Alli was a prominent subsidiser of Starmer's expenses, as revealed in the Register of Members' Interests.

Rachel Reeves wanted to extract more in tax revenue from so-called 'non-doms', people living in the UK but registered to pay tax elsewhere and not paying UK tax on earnings abroad. Her predecessor as chancellor, Jeremy Hunt, had legislated to end non-dom status; but Labour wanted to remove remaining concessions and spend an anticipated £1 billion of extra revenue on NHS appointments and school breakfast clubs. Amid warnings of non-doms leaving the UK and gloomy forecasts from the Office for Budget Responsibility, there were rumours that the non-dom pot might prove to be an empty vessel.

28 September 2024
Andy Davey
Daily Telegraph

29 September 2024
Dave Simonds
Observer

On 26 September 2024, Sir Keir Starmer and Foreign Secretary David Lammy were in New York, at the United Nations. They also found time to meet Donald Trump over dinner. Since winning its landslide victory in the July general election, Labour had been buffeted over expenses, the winter fuel payment and fears of a new era of austerity. Accordingly, Labour's poll ratings had slumped markedly. But a breezy Trump, ahead of their dinner, described Starmer as 'very nice' and 'popular'. Starmer pronounced himself 'a great believer in personal relations on the international stage'.

The Conservative Party's three-day conference opened on 29 September 2024. Following the battering the party had received in the July general election, it was a chance for the four remaining candidates hoping to replace Rishi Sunak as leader to shine before the assembled delegates. By a strange or not so strange coincidence, that week also witnessed publicity for and excerpts from ex-prime minister Boris Johnson's forthcoming political memoir, *Unleashed*. In the blunt appraisal of the *Guardian*, Johnson wished to remind the four contenders that 'he is the election-winning Tory colossus that they can only dream of being'.

30 September 2024
Nicola Jennings
Guardian

Aspiring Conservative leader Kemi Badenoch lived up to her reputation for outspokenness when she told Times Radio that maternity pay was 'excessive' because it was a 'function of tax': 'we're taking from one group of people and giving it to another'. Her Conservative challengers quickly disagreed. Robert Jenrick thought 'our maternity pay is among the lowest in the OECD', James Cleverly emphasised childcare costs, and Tom Tugendhat thought 'maternity and paternity care are very important'. Badenoch moved into damage-limitation mode, posting on X (Twitter) that while 'the burden of regulation on business' had gone too far, 'of course' she believed in maternity pay.

1 October 2024
Ben Jennings
Guardian

On 2 October 2024, the four Conservative leadership challengers made their last speeches to conference, seeking the affections of the party faithful. Reactions suggested that the centrist James Cleverly, appealing for Conservatives to be 'more normal', had the biggest impact. Yet, in a YouGov Poll of 802 party members taken the previous week, he and Tom Tugendhat had only commanded 16% of votes, trailing Robert Jenrick (24%) and Kemi Badenoch (27%). Trounced by Labour in the general election and facing a Reform UK challenge on the right, whoever won would be unlikely to experience plain sailing.

3 October 2024
Dave Brown
Independent

5 October 2024
Andy Davey
Daily Telegraph

After long-running international discussions, and under pressure from an International Court of Justice ruling, the Labour government agreed to transfer sovereignty of the Chagos Islands, including Diego Garcia (with its UK–US military base), to Mauritius. There was immediate uproar. Ex-foreign secretary James Cleverly called Labour 'weak, weak, weak', before it was pointed out that he had initiated negotiations in 2022; his supporters blamed the prime minister at the time, Liz Truss. As the cartoonist observed, then 'Liz Truss hit out at claims that she had been responsible . . . and claimed it had been Boris Johnson's fault.'

As the UK approached the 100-day milestone of Labour in power and Sir Keir Starmer in the driving seat, the heady days of the party's crushing victory at the general election seemed a long way off and Labour's brief political honeymoon well and truly over. Were the wheels coming off? The cartoonist noted that 'the *Economist* still insist that their political cartoons should be in black and white. Very few UK newspapers do: this is a pity, because it suits political cartoons very well. We're dealing with a simplified and stark world view. And a black-and-white image can be much more powerful.'

10 October 2024
Peter Schrank
Economist

Boris Johnson's memoir *Unleashed* was officially published on 10 October 2024. In typically Johnsonian style, it blended pithy description and humour with forthright opinions and reflections. The book ranged from his days as London mayor through Brexit and his turbulent prime ministership, including, of course, the Covid-19 pandemic – and the 'Partygate' breaches of lockdown and social-distancing rules at Number 10. He now regretted his previous apologies over Partygate as 'pathetic' and 'grovelling'. The National Covid Memorial Wall in London, along the Thames, features painted hearts for victims of the pandemic.

10 October 2024
Ben Jennings
i

Labour's economic challenge was squaring the circle of manifesto promises not to raise taxes with plans to 'invest', and a commitment to stay within self-declared 'fiscal rules' that borrowing would not fund day-to-day spending; and then there was the £22 billion 'black hole' of debt that Labour claimed was a Conservative legacy. According to the cartoonist, 'Reeves's pledge to protect government spending while paying off debt put her on course for a record tax-raising budget – or failure.' It seemed an uphill battle. In Rev. W. Awdry's *Thomas the Tank Engine* children's classics, the anthropomorphised trains often had to puff up steep gradients.

11 October 2024
Andy Davey
Daily Telegraph

12 October 2024
Dave Brown
Independent

The final round of leadership voting among Conservative MPs delivered a shock: frontrunner James Cleverly was knocked out, as was Tom Tugendhat. 'How on earth did that happen?' asked the BBC's political editor, Chris Mason. 'How the hell did it happen, and what does it mean?' asked the *Guardian*. What was certain was that Kemi Badenoch and Robert Jenrick were left in the battle to be leader of a party whose very survival some doubted. The cartoonist was inspired by the painter Pieter Bruegel the Elder, whose work included the gruesome *The Triumph of Death*, featuring a dog chewing on a baby.

On 14 October 2024, Health Secretary Wes Streeting wrote in the *Daily Telegraph* that an obesity epidemic placed a 'significant burden' on the NHS and cost the economy £11 billion a year. He announced new investment and collaboration with a pharmaceutical company to tackle obesity, including giving weight-loss jabs to help people 'get back to work'. A backlash prompted Streeting to deny he meant 'some dystopian future where I involuntarily jab unemployed people who are overweight'. The Conservatives' 'Labour Isn't Working' poster, with its queue of unemployed people, was deployed for the 1979 general election and has been reconceived regularly by cartoonists.

16 October 2024
Patrick Blower
Daily Telegraph

Fears of what Rachel Reeves might deliver in the end-of-the-month Budget were mounting, as she continued to emphasise her stark inheritance. The £22 billion 'black hole' of debt was, she insisted, not a one-off but an annual debt, so that every year in the short term that hole would need to be filled. If she was not going to loosen her fiscal rules, which limited borrowing to capital investment, then spending cuts and/or higher taxation looked likely, possibly (according to Reuters' and other estimates) amounting to £40 billion. Either option suggested Labour promises were in danger.

17 October 2024
Nicola Jennings
Guardian

On 16 October 2024, it was announced that ex-Chelsea FC manager Thomas Tuchel would take over from Gareth Southgate as England team manager in 2025. At the same time, Lord (Mervyn) King, the former governor of the Bank of England, wrote an open letter to the *Independent* with advice and encouragement for his one-time employee, Rachel Reeves. 'Your generation is now in charge,' he observed, so he advised Reeves to be 'courageous' and 'bold' and resist 'the political compromises that others will urge on you'. 'Be ruthlessly honest with the public,' he said, but 'resist the temptation to fiddle with the tax system.'

17 October 2024
Dave Brown
Independent

18 October 2024
Peter Brookes
The Times

On 16 October 2024, an Israeli military patrol in Gaza chanced upon a high-value target in the city of Rafah. As the cartoonist explained: 'The Hamas leader Yahya Sinwar, the mastermind behind the 7 October attack, was killed by Israeli forces, who then continued their relentless bombardment of Gaza. I had a hellish time with my cartoon as this news arrived so close to my deadline. I had drawn Biden haranguing Netanyahu over a different aspect of his Gaza policy but was able to change the caption to take in Israel eliminating Sinwar, which was the bigger story.'

In an effort to connect with 'ordinary' voters, Donald Trump popped up at a McDonald's restaurant in a swing county of Pennsylvania, where he served French fries and spoke to the media. The event took place on the birthday of Democratic rival Kamala Harris, who had been harking back to her student days earning money at the fast-food chain. The company insisted that 'McDonald's does not endorse candidates for elected office' and emphasised that accepting Trump's request was the franchise owner's decision. But the company added: 'We open our doors to everyone.' McDonald's eponymous symbol is Ronald McDonald – a clown.

22 October 2024
Patrick Blower
Daily Telegraph

24 October 2024
Peter Brookes
The Times

Trump's campaign team filed a complaint to the US Federal Election Commission about 'blatant foreign interference', because some Labour Party activists were supporting Harris's bid. Meanwhile, billionaire Elon Musk dramatically upped his payments to random Pennsylvania voters to sign a petition for 'free speech and the right to bear arms'. According to the cartoonist, 'Elon Musk was doing a lottery-style giveaway of $1 million per day to registered voters in swing states. Of course, it was interference from abroad that was a big point of discussion . . . But I wanted it to be about interference full stop, which is what Musk had basically done . . .'

Britain's history as a slave-trading power continued to have modern repercussions, as the heads of Commonwealth nations prepared for their biennial meeting, which took place in Samoa. Increasing numbers of Commonwealth nations were pushing for serious discussions on reparations, putting the UK under pressure. Sir Keir Starmer described the slave trade as 'abhorrent' and said 'an apology has already been made' while resisting financial reparations for decisions made in previous centuries.

25 October 2024
Dave Brown
Independent

27 October 2024
Chris Riddell
Observer

In interviews with the *New York Times* and the *Atlantic*, General John F. Kelly, who was once Donald Trump's White House chief of staff (July 2017 to January 2019), offered stark warnings should Trump be re-elected to the US presidency. 'He's certainly an authoritarian' who 'admires people who are dictators' was Kelly's view. He remembered upbraiding Trump when, on 'multiple' occasions, the president had praised Hitler. 'Project 2025' was the colloquial name for a set of radical, populist right-of-centre polices advocated by the Heritage Foundation think tank. Opponents of Trump feared that he wanted to put them into practice.

30 October 2024 was UK Budget day. For the cartoonist, 'Budgets can be tricky . . . I didn't have a great deal of time to do my cartoon, because Rachel Reeves's speech was quite long . . . Then you have to put your thoughts together . . . on the day, it's always much harder to get to grips with what's in it. This cartoon doesn't do that: it's a generalised comment. It was Halloween, so . . . I've drawn all these ghastly, scary measures that Reeves produced. Some of them, like raising duties on private jets, were fine by me.' In the event, the headline was £40 billion of extra tax revenue, notably an increase in employers' National Insurance contributions.

31 October 2024
Peter Brookes
The Times

1 November 2024
Ben Jennings
Guardian

The two sides in the US presidential election traded blows after a comedian at a Trump rally characterised Puerto Rico as 'a floating island of garbage'. An angry President Biden then told Latino voters: 'the only garbage I see floating out there is his supporters' – though it was transcribed as 'supporter's', singular – before adding 'demonisation of Latinos'. Eager to exploit Biden's gaffe, Trump flew into the battleground state of Wisconsin, donned high-vis and mounted the cab of a refuse truck 'in honour of Kamala and Joe Biden', telling the media that '250 million Americans are not garbage'.

The leadership of the Conservative Party was finally decided with the victory of Kemi Badenoch, who won nearly 12,500 more votes than her remaining rival, Robert Jenrick, in the poll of nearly 132,000 party members. Welcoming her, Sir Keir Starmer posted on X: 'The first Black leader of a Westminster party is a proud moment for our country.' Boris Johnson looked forward to her bringing 'a much-needed zing and zap'. Badenoch promised to 'renew' her party, but there was no denying that the bruised and battered Conservatives had ripped through six leaders in little more than eight years.

3 November 2024
Andy Davey
Sunday Telegraph

As election day arrived in the United States, the candidates appeared to be neck and neck. 'US braces as two starkly opposing visions clash' was the BBC's Sarah Smith's summary, as each campaign warned of catastrophe should the other win. One stark difference was Trump's dismissal of climate change and global warming as 'one of the greatest scams of all time', backed by promises to 'drill, baby, drill', and so open up the United States to increased fossil-fuel extraction. On this issue, the differences between the candidates were, in the view of one climate scientist interviewed by the *Guardian*, 'night and day'.

4 November 2024
Ella Baron
Guardian

In the end, the US presidential election was a triumph for the Trump campaign, as Democratic hopes turned to despondency overnight when Trump won all the crucial swing states. Moreover, he won the popular vote by some 2 million votes, and Republicans toppled enough Democrats to take control of both the House of Representatives and the Senate. Trump celebrated what he called his 'unprecedented and powerful mandate', while Harris exited the stage promising a 'peaceful' transfer of power, even if 'many people feel like we are entering a dark time'.

7 November 2024
Ella Baron
Guardian

8 November 2024
Peter Brookes
The Times

Whether out of trepidation, enthusiasm or simply diplomatic protocol, world leaders rushed to congratulate Donald Trump on his re-election. Two of the first were Benjamin Netanyahu and Sir Keir Starmer, both citing Trump's 'historic' victory. The cartoonist was not impressed: 'Just after Donald Trump was elected, everyone was sucking up to him. It was disgraceful . . . calling up one after the other as quickly as they could, trying to be the first to talk to him – even Keir Starmer. Everyone was trying to get in there, doing exactly what's shown in the cartoon. I wanted to be literal, and I was.'

On 13 November 2024, Justin Welby, Archbishop of Canterbury, announced his resignation. He had been resisting calls to stand down, but now admitted he had to take 'personal and institutional responsibility' for failing to follow up rigorously enough on reports of physical and sexual abuse against boys carried out at Christian camps, since the 1980s, by barrister John Smyth. Keith Makin, who led the independent review into the Church's handling of allegations, said that 'despite the efforts of some individuals to bring the abuse to the attention of authorities, the responses by the Church of England and others were wholly ineffective and amounted to a cover-up'.

14 November 2024
Dave Brown
Independent

14 November 2024
Nicola Jennings
Guardian

Massive cuts to federal budgets were on the agenda, as President-Elect Trump appointed his energetic billionaire supporter Elon Musk as co-lead of a new Department of Government Efficiency. Technically, it would be advisory and 'outside of government'. The Tesla founder Musk tweeted on his X platform that there would be 'a leaderboard for most insanely dumb spending of your tax dollars', with results that would be 'extremely tragic and extremely entertaining'. Trump estimated that $2 trillion could be cut. Critics wondered about Musk's objectivity, given his many business interests, some of which received federal funding.

In another controversial appointment, Trump picked Robert F. Kennedy, Jr as his new health secretary. The son of Democratic Party legend Robert F. Kennedy and nephew of President John F. Kennedy, he had rejected his family's politics and pursued conspiracy-theory-fuelled campaigns on public health. He abandoned an independent run for president in order to back Trump. In the cartoonist's view, 'RFK is an anti-vaxer and a complete idiot. I found two quotes, one from JFK and one from RFK Jr, that seemed to work very well together.' When the editor of this collection tweeted the cartoon, RFK Jr replied: 'Thank you for your support.'

16 November 2024
Peter Brookes
The Times

On 15 November 2024, the same day that the BBC broadcast the annual Children in Need fundraising appeal, the Office for National Statistics released sobering figures on the UK's economic health. Growth in the third quarter of the year had actually fallen, to 0.1 per cent, from 0.5 per cent in the second quarter. And exports continued to fall, too. 'I am not satisfied with these figures,' said Rachel Reeves, as she insisted economic growth was 'at the heart' of all her plans. Conservative critics accused her of squandering a legacy of higher growth bequeathed by the previous Conservative administration.

16 November 2024
Christian Adams
Daily Telegraph

Trump's cabinet nominations did not lack for colourful characters. Commentators noted that, for his second presidency, Trump seemed keen to reward ideological bedfellows who could be 'disruptors'. He nominated Tulsi Gabbard – once accused of being a Putin apologist – as director of national intelligence, and Fox News anchor Pete Hegseth as defense secretary. Most startling was the choice of Representative Matt Gaetz as attorney general: he was under investigation by the House Ethics Committee for alleged sex- and drugs-related activities. The most eye-catching insurrectionist to storm the Capitol on 6 January 2021 was the so-called 'QAnon Shaman', who wore horned bearskin headgear.

17 November 2024
Chris Riddell
Observer

After reports that Ukraine was finally allowed to use US-supplied long-range missiles for a strike inside Russia, Vladimir Putin announced changes to Russia's nuclear doctrine. In a clear effort to deter Ukraine's allies, he stated that Russia might respond with nuclear weapons if attacked with conventional weapons by a power that was itself supported by a nuclear-armed state. While raising the spectre of death for millions, Putin was believed to be an enthusiastic injector of Botox to maintain his youthful skin. In the film *Hellraiser* (1987) and its sequels, 'Pinhead' is the evil, otherworldly character with the distinctive nail-studded head.

21 November 2024
Ben Jennings
Guardian

Labour's plans to subject farms worth more than £1 million to potential inheritance tax had attracted a backlash from farmers and rural populations. On 19 November 2024, around 13,000 protesters gathered in Whitehall, while 1,800 farmers lobbied MPs outside Westminster. Supporting them was ex-*Top Gear* presenter and controversialist Jeremy Clarkson, who now owned a farm called Diddly Squat, as featured in his TV programme *Clarkson's Farm*. He had already called on the government to recognise it had 'cocked this one up'. Since 2018, Clarkson had hosted the ITV quiz show *Who Wants to Be a Millionaire?*

22 November 2024
Graeme Bandeira
Northern Agenda

On 25–26 November 2024, the UK hosted a NATO Cyber Defence Conference. For the government, Pat McFadden, chancellor of the Duchy of Lancaster, made a widely trailed speech containing stark warnings about Russian threats, highlighting cyber-attacks on Ukraine, and calling for a united response. 'Here in the UK,' he said, 'Russia has targeted our media, our telecoms, our political and democratic institutions, and our energy infrastructure.' At the same time, Storm Bert was bringing widespread flooding to the UK, while Lord Darzi's independent report on the NHS described the health service as being in 'critical condition'.

25 November 2024
Patrick Blower
Daily Telegraph

President-Elect Trump was also issuing stark warnings about what he would do when taking office on 20 January 2025. In his words, he planned 'many' executive orders, and among the first he would 'sign all necessary documents to charge Mexico and Canada a 25% tariff on ALL products' entering the United States. He added that he would be 'charging China an additional 10% Tariff, above any additional tariffs'. His ostensible justification was punishing these countries for not curbing illegal traffic in the opioid painkiller fentanyl, which had caused tens of thousands of deadly overdoses in the United States.

29 November 2024
Kevin Kallaugher
Economist

By the time the Advent countdown to Christmas began, Sir Keir Starmer had suffered his first Cabinet loss when his transport secretary resigned. Louise Haigh's position became untenable when it emerged she had pleaded guilty to fraud committed (but was later conditionally discharged) in 2013 after claiming the loss of a work-supplied mobile phone during a mugging. She now said it was an honest mistake, having only later discovered she still had the phone, and having been badly advised to plead guilty. She insisted she had informed Starmer in 2020. Conservatives pushed him to 'explain this obvious failure of judgement' in appointing Haigh.

1 December 2024
Christian Adams
Sunday Telegraph

According to the cartoonist, 'Things had been leaked from Starmer's forthcoming "Plan for Change" speech. Number 10 didn't want us to think it was a "relaunch", but it was. My point here was that Labour had achieved very little in voters' minds, although they argued they'd achieved a lot ... The mistakes and the missteps were more plentiful than the successes. Relaunching the *Titanic* when it's already sunk was an image that quickly came to my mind.' A forthcoming documentary from *National Geographic* and Atlantic Productions was charting work to reconstruct the famous liner digitally.

2 December 2024
Peter Brookes
The Times

3 December 2024
Ben Jennings
Guardian

On 1 December 2024, Joe Biden conferred a 'full and unconditional' presidential pardon on his son Hunter, who in 2018 was found guilty of unlawfully buying a handgun, and who was now awaiting sentence for tax evasion. Biden's justification was that Hunter was the victim of 'selective prosecution', after 'several of my political opponents in Congress instigated [the charges] to attack me'. Biden had promised not to interfere in judicial processes, and in now doing so he gave succour to Trump, who claimed that his own felony conviction in May 2024, for covering up hush money, was a political attack.

According to the cartoonist, 'When I was drawing this, it wasn't at all clear what had happened to Bashar al-Assad, Syria's president for 24 years, who had been toppled by rebels. There was a lot of confusion through the day, so it was very difficult to do a direct cartoon about Syria. I liked making this link between that story and Reform UK, which that week had overtaken Labour in the polls for the first time.' Nigel Farage posted on X: 'We can change the future of British politics. The sky is our limit.'

9 December 2024
Peter Brookes
The Times

13 December 2024
Kevin Kallaugher
Economist

Assad's regime in Syria collapsed on 8 December 2024, in the face of a short but concerted advance by opposition forces in the country's civil war. The mystery of Assad's whereabouts was solved by the revelation that he had been whisked away to Russia: Vladimir Putin's military backing had done much in recent years to prop up Assad's tenuous hold on Syria. Analysts suggested that the two authoritarian leaders were not at all close, but the Kremlin indicated that the rescue was Putin's personal decision. Now, Assad joined assorted other exiles in Russia, beyond the reach of international justice.

As part of Labour's 'Plan for Change', Sir Keir Starmer promised 1.5 million new homes in five years. As the cartoonist commented: 'Starmer vowed to override "blockers" standing in the way of building.' Angela Rayner also insisted she would 'not hesitate to do what it takes to … deliver the biggest boost in social and affordable housing in a generation'. Not only would councils need to set mandatory house-building targets, but they would also be required to reassess green-belt land, normally preserved from development, to identify which parts of it could be reclassified, in Rayner's words, as 'low-quality grey belt'.

13 December 2024
Andy Davey
Daily Telegraph

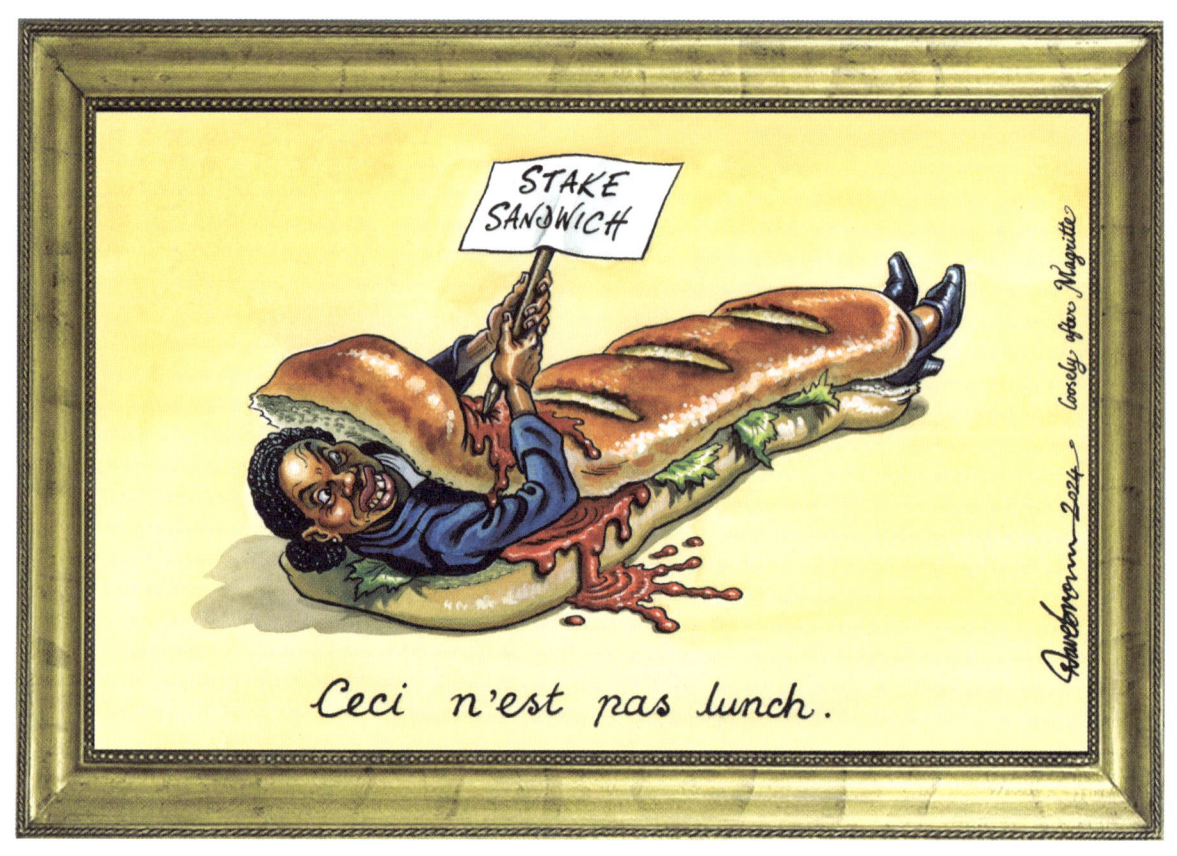

14 December 2024
Dave Brown
Independent

In an interview with the *Spectator*, Kemi Badenoch described lunchbreaks as being 'for wimps'. 'I have food brought in and I work and eat at the same time,' she declared. Moreover, sandwiches were not 'real food' and she would 'not touch bread if it's moist'. But sometimes, she acknowledged, she hankered after red meat and would 'get a steak'. A spokesperson for Number 10 remarked that Sir Keir Starmer did not need steaks brought in and was 'quite happy' with sandwiches. In 1929, Magritte painted a smoker's pipe with the inscription *ceci n'est pas une pipe* ('this is not a pipe').

Prince Andrew's friends again came under intense scrutiny when a 'semi-secret national court' (as the BBC described it) confirmed a decision to ban a Chinese businessman, revealed as Yang Tengbo, from the UK. Yang was allegedly involved with China's United Front Work Department, which diffuses Chinese Communist Party power globally, including by cultivating prominent individuals deemed susceptible to influence. In 2020, a royal advisor had assured Yang that his relationship with Andrew put him 'at the top of a tree that many, many people would like to be on'. The prince's office denied that anything 'of a sensitive nature' was ever discussed.

17 December 2024
Ben Jennings
Guardian

Since 2015, the Women Against State Pension Inequality (WASPI) had argued that women born in the 1950s had been discriminated against by decisions to raise women's state pension age to 65 – and then accelerate those changes. Lack of information, they argued, had left women badly out of pocket. But the government now rejected an ombudsman's recommendation for compensation, relying on the finding that 90 per cent of women had a 'vague awareness' of general changes afoot regarding pension changes. Sir Keir Starmer said 'taxpayers simply can't afford' £10.5 billion of compensation. Discontented backbenchers felt the 'WASPI women' had been betrayed.

19 December 2024
Dave Brown
Independent

After meeting with Elon Musk at Donald Trump's Mar-a-Lago resort, Nigel Farage did little to dampen speculation that Musk might put his wallet behind Reform UK. 'We can do great things together,' Farage felt, and later referred to 'ongoing negotiations' about financial support. The cartoonist commented: 'I dislike drawing politicians as animals. It rarely works. But Farage makes a very good frog. And he would make a great toad. I'd love to draw him as Mr Toad from *The Wind in the Willows*. Perhaps I'd better copyright that idea before another cartoonist does it. Unless it's already been done . . .'

20 December 2024
Peter Schrank
The Times

21 December 2024
Christian Adams
Daily Telegraph

On 20 December 2024, Number 10 Downing Street confirmed the Labour grandee Lord (Peter) Mandelson as 'the next British Ambassador to the United States of America' and lauded his 'extensive foreign and economic policy knowledge'. The ex-minister and ex-EU trade commissioner had, some years earlier, described Donald Trump as a 'bully' and 'little short of a white nationalist and racist', whom even his admirers thought 'reckless and a danger to the world'. Sources in Trump's circle described the appointment of Lord Mandelson as 'horrible' and even called him a 'moron'. Frank Capra's *Mr Smith Goes to Washington* (1939) is a Hollywood classic.

A Christmas-time spat broke out between Reform UK and the Conservatives. With a digital counter on his party's website, Nigel Farage trumpeted the number of Reform members on Boxing Day as surpassing the Conservative membership of 131,680 (as recently revealed for the leadership vote). Kemi Badenoch ridiculed the digital tally as a 'fake . . . coded to tick up automatically'. The cartoonist was 'not quite happy with my caricature of Kemi Badenoch here. Why did she have to stop wearing her glasses? We cartoonists love a prop.'

28 December 2024
Peter Schrank
The Times

30 December 2024
Andy Davey
Daily Telegraph

Describing his image, the cartoonist explained: 'A Republican rift opens between the Silicon Valley "Tech Right", which wants to import skilled workers to the US on restrictive H-1B visas, and "America First" MAGA loyalists.' Elon Musk waded into an argument about the H-1B visa programme by saying he would even 'go to war' to defend it against 'hateful, unrepentant' racists in the Republican Party. In his view, it was vital for attracting, among others, top engineers. Critics claimed the visas held down wages for US citizens in equivalent roles, and the 'Make America Great Again' base was generally hostile to immigration.

The rancour of US politics was interrupted on 29 December 2024 when, at the age of 100, Jimmy Carter died. The Nobel Prize winner and 39th president of the United States endured a troubled presidency, beset with crises, which ensured he only served one term. But he spent the next 40 years deeply engaged in humanitarian causes. President Biden urged young people to 'study Jimmy Carter, a man of principle, faith and humility'. The cartoonist noted: 'When an important person dies, we often draw something respectful, possibly a bit bland. In this instance, I was motivated to give the cartoon some contemporary relevance.'

31 December 2024
Peter Schrank
The Times

31 December 2024
Andy Davey
Daily Telegraph

As 2024 concluded, whatever remained of Labour's Christmas cheer was doused by a so-called 'mega-poll' conducted by the *Sunday Times*. Extrapolated from more than 11,000 voters, it suggested that if a general election were held imminently, Labour would be reduced to 228 seats and the Conservatives would climb to 222 seats. In addition, Reform UK would replace the Liberal Democrats as the third party by massively increasing its tally to 72 seats. As the cartoonist put it: 'The first major analysis after the election presents a fresh blow to Starmer and his rocky start. Bad weather too.'

Health Secretary Wes Streeting announced a new independent commission to assess reforms for the social-care sector, amid dire warnings that the current system was on its knees. This followed the chancellor's decision not to implement earlier reforms, because of cost – reforms that were themselves delayed by the previous Conservative government. And now the new commission, under Baroness Casey, was not due to make its final recommendations until 2028. DC Comics' Superman (aka journalist Clark Kent) once transformed into his costume in a phone box, after which the association between phone boxes and the superhero became indelible.

4 January 2025
Ben Jennings
i Paper

7 January 2025
Peter Songi
Guardian

Elon Musk used his X platform to launch inflammatory interventions in British politics. When the government resisted a new investigation into historical sexual abuse in Oldham, Musk called the safeguarding minister, Jess Phillips, a 'rape genocide apologist' who should be 'in prison'. Musk then decided Nigel Farage did not 'have what it takes' to lead Reform UK, while Farage distanced himself from Musk's calls to have the far-right Tommy Robinson (Stephen Yaxley-Lennon) released from his jail sentence for contempt of court. Without naming Musk, on 6 January the prime minister condemned those 'spreading lies and misinformation'.

Mark Zuckerberg, the CEO of social-media behemoth Meta (including Facebook, Instagram and Threads), announced that the company would discard fact checkers in favour of user-generated 'community notes similar to X'. Meta would now prioritise 'free speech' and roll back 'the amount of censorship on our platforms', even if 'we're going to catch less bad stuff'. In other changes, Meta's moderation team would move from California, with its liberal reputation, to Texas, and its new president of global affairs was a well-known Republican, Joel Kaplan. The changes were viewed as an obvious attempt to curry favour with the incoming Trump presidency.

8 January 2025
Nicola Jennings
Guardian

Lawyers for Liz Truss sent a 'cease and desist' letter to the current prime minister, demanding that he stop saying she had had 'crashed the economy' during her days at Number 10. She thought 'defamatory' remarks had caused 'serious harm to her reputation', and she implicitly blamed them for the loss of her once-impregnable South West Norfolk seat to Labour. The economic and political fallout of the so-called 'mini-budget' in 2022 had swiftly ended Truss's prime ministership: a spokesman for Starmer suggested that Truss's time would be better spent apologising to 'millions of people' whose mortgage payments rose in its aftermath.

10 January 2025
Dave Brown
Independent

According to the cartoonist, 'Economists warned that the government was "on course" to miss its own budget borrowing targets after interest rates for UK long-term borrowing rose to their highest levels this century. A Treasury spokesman claimed markets "continue to function in an orderly way".' The Treasury added that 'meeting the fiscal rules is non-negotiable and the government will have an iron grip on the public finances'. Given the sell off in the bond markets, the Institute for Fiscal Studies suggested that further tax rises or spending cuts might be needed.

10 January 2025
Andy Davey
Daily Telegraph

As UK borrowing costs surged but the value of the pound shrank, Rachel Reeves and the governor of the Bank of England headed to China. Meeting the Chinese vice-premier, Reeves said she was in the country to 'unlock tangible benefits for British businesses' and to 'ensure we have greater access to the second-largest economy in the world'. Her political opponents did not see it that way. The Conservative shadow chancellor described her as 'missing in action', while his colleague Tom Tugendhat said that, given the market turbulence, it looked like 'she's going with a begging bowl, not with a trading deal'.

11 January 2025
Christian Adams
Daily Telegraph

As wildfires devastated suburbs of Los Angeles, a blame game erupted. Donald Trump attacked California's Democratic governor, Gavin Newsom (whom he called 'Newscum'), for failing to redirect water in Northern California to the south. Newsom thought Trump's grasp of the issue was 'pure fiction' and accused him of 'spreading disinformation from the sidelines', saying that the real problem was the fires' effect on pumping mechanisms and electrical supply, not the supply of water. Meanwhile, the *Guardian* estimated that tech moguls had injected more than $273 million into Trump's presidential campaign, most of it from Elon Musk.

13 January 2025
Ella Baron
Guardian

14 January 2025
Ben Jennings
Guardian

President-Elect Trump stoked further controversy, and a backlash, with his ambitions to take over Greenland. Speaking to the media at his Mar-a-Lago complex, Trump insisted that US ownership of Greenland was needed for world peace and for tracking Russian and Chinese ships, and that both Greenland and the Panama Canal were vital for US 'economic security'. Moreover, when asked if he ruled out military takeovers, he replied: 'No, I can't assure you.' Múte Egede, prime minister of Greenland's 57,000 people, said that while the autonomous territory sought independence from Denmark, it was not putting itself up for sale to another country.

At Prime Minister's Questions on 15 January, Sir Keir Starmer defended Labour's economic policy. Kemi Badenoch, on the attack after a tax-raising Budget, commented: 'The prime minister refused to repeat his chancellor's promise that she wouldn't come back for more.' She asked: 'Will he now rule out any new tax rises this year?' He replied: 'We can't just tax our way out of the problems they left us' and doubled down, too, on sticking to Labour's 'fiscal rules'. That raised fears that the chancellor might take the axe to government spending instead.

16 January 2025
Dave Brown
Independent

Labour's moves to repeal parts of the 2023 Northern Ireland Troubles (Legacy and Reconciliation) Act could, it was reported, allow the ex-Sinn Féin president Gerry Adams to claim financial compensation. The controversial Act attempted to draw a line under legacy issues from Northern Ireland's Troubles; but provisions were inserted to stop Adams receiving any compensation due him after the Supreme Court quashed his old convictions for attempted prison escapes. When a 2024 High Court ruling declared parts of the Act incompatible with the European Convention on Human Rights, the path to Adams's compensation seemed to be opening up again.

16 January 2025
Patrick Blower
Daily Telegraph

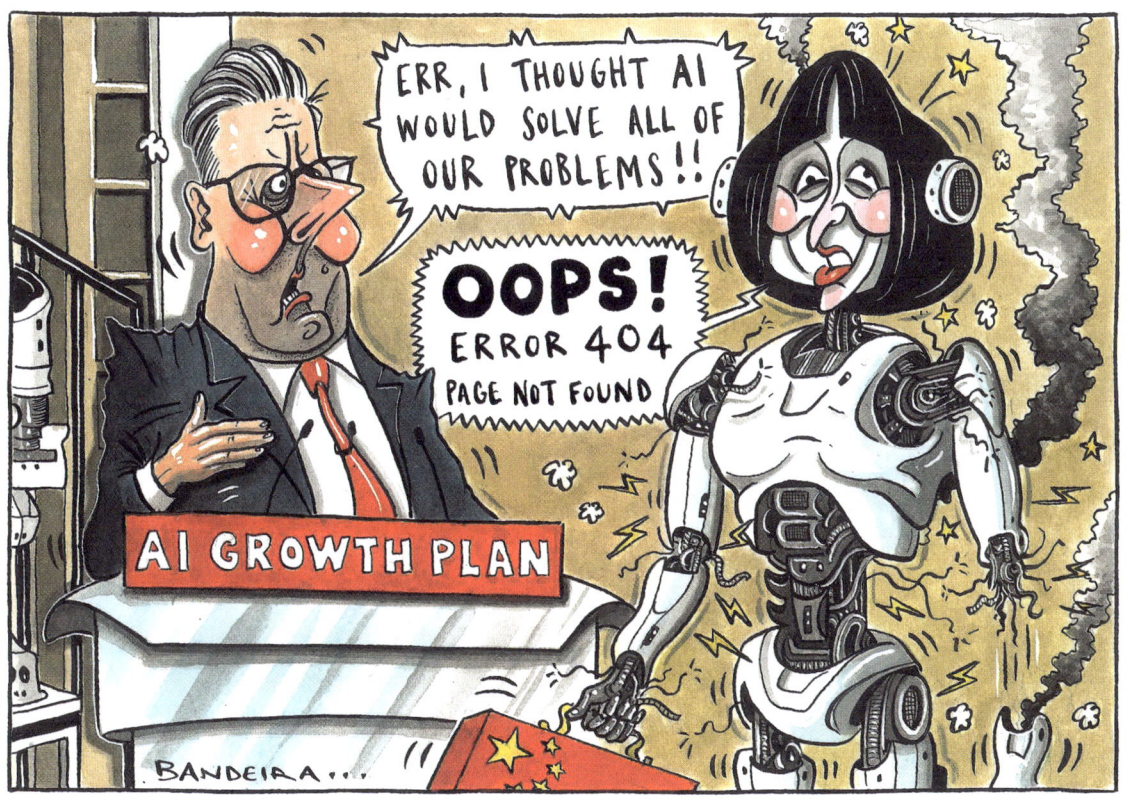

On 13 January, Sir Keir Starmer unveiled the government's adoption of a 50-point 'AI Opportunities Action Plan'. According to his office's bold press release, 'artificial intelligence will be unleashed across the UK to deliver a decade of national renewal', and so, in Starmer's words, 'we must move fast and take action to win the global race'. He trumpeted the potential economic benefits of AI, in terms of growth and productivity. At the same time, pressure was mounting on his beleaguered chancellor, fresh from a trip to China. He said she had his 'confidence', but Conservatives described her as 'hanging on by her fingernails'.

17 January 2025
Graeme Bandeira
Northern Agenda

19 January 2025
Nicola Jennings
Guardian

With ferocious winter weather hitting Washington, DC, the inauguration-day rituals for Donald Trump as the 47th US president were to be moved indoors, inside the Capitol's rotunda. As president-elect, Trump had already declared: 'Everybody wants to be my friend!!!' It was already clear that a group of tech billionaires – the so-called 'tech bros' – would be invited guests. In the end, Mark Zuckerberg, Elon Musk and Amazon's Jeff Bezos were joined by Apple's Tim Cook and Google's Sundar Pichai in seating arrangements that gave them prominence even over Trump's cabinet members. Senior Democrats warned of a billionaire oligarchy running the United States.

The long-running legal battle between Prince Harry and News Group Newspapers ended on 22 January with an NGN apology and a rumoured £10 million in damages. The 'full and unequivocal apology' was, in NGN's statement, 'for the serious intrusion by *The Sun* between 1996 and 2011 into his private life' and 'unlawful activities carried out by private investigators working for *The Sun*', as well as for phone-hacking conducted by the *News of the World*. When John Major and the Conservatives were unexpectedly voted back into power in April 1992, the *Sun* claimed the credit with the headline 'It's the *Sun* wot won it'.

23 January 2025
Ben Jennings
Guardian

24 January 2025
Andy Davey
Daily Telegraph

At the World Economic Forum in Davos, Switzerland, Rachel Reeves said she had 'listened to concerns of the non-dom community' regarding measures to clamp down on their tax exemptions. Now, non-doms could enjoy a 12 per cent tax rate for two years, instead of the 45 per cent maximum income-tax rate, and an extended 'repatriation' facility would encourage them to bring foreign assets to the UK. 'Rachel Reeves Regrets!' noted the cartoonist. 'Apparently, too many millionaire tax evaders fled the country . . . She wants to say "sorry" and ask them back in. After all, we want more patriotic, committed people like that, eh?'

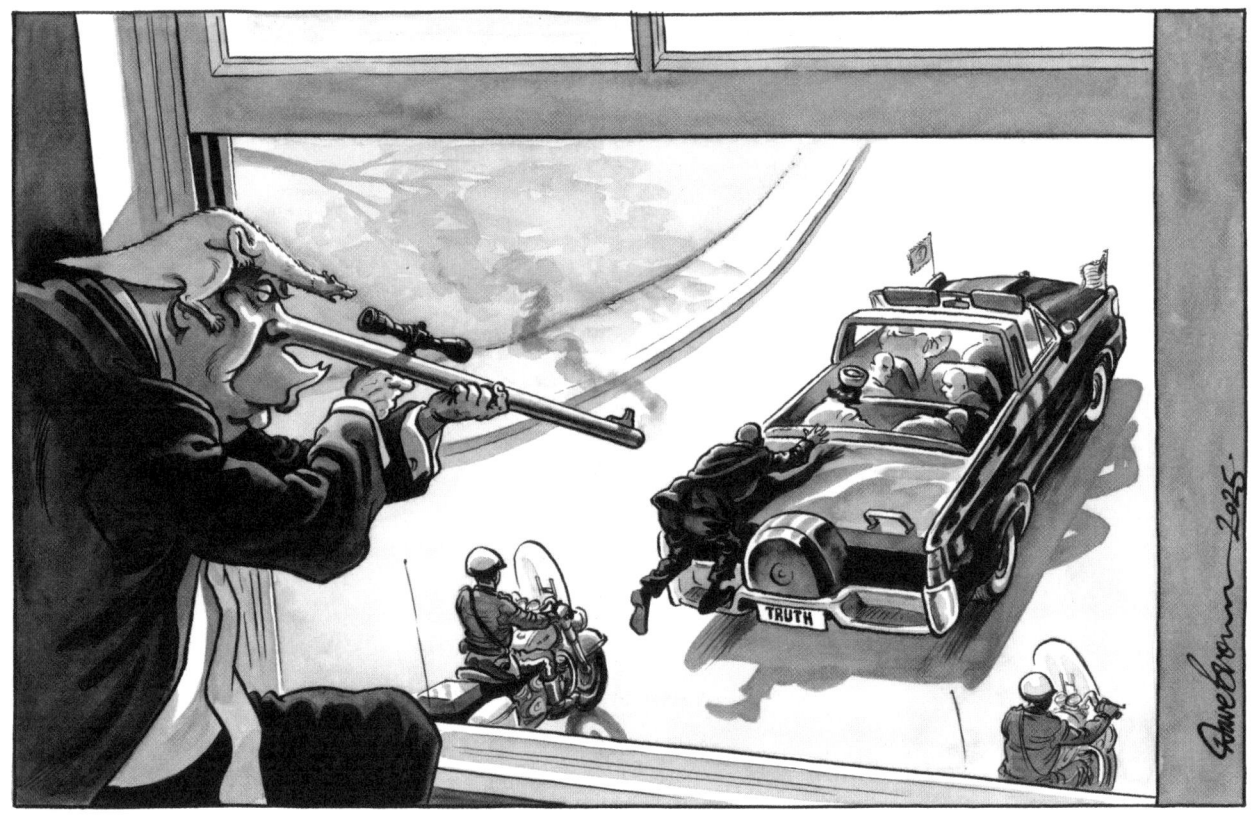

Among the flurry of executive orders that President Trump set about signing was one to release the remaining records about three notorious assassinations: of the civil rights leader Martin Luther King, Jr and the Democratic presidential candidate Robert (Bobby) Kennedy, both killed in 1968; and of Robert's elder brother, President John F. Kennedy, shot in his motorcade in Dallas in 1963. 'That's a big one, huh?' commented Trump, adding, 'Everything will be revealed'. To some critics, it was truth itself, and Trump's casual disregard for facts and evidence, that was the likely victim of his ascendancy.

25 January 2025
Dave Brown
Independent

25 January 2025
Christian Adams
Daily Telegraph

Ed Miliband, energy secretary, found himself in an awkward spot when it looked like cabinet colleagues would back the expansion of Heathrow airport as part of the economic growth agenda. In 2018, Miliband had voted against expansion, because 'we owe it to future generations not just to have good environmental principles but to act on them'. Now, quizzed on whether he might resign in protest, he described the idea as 'ridiculous' because he was working on 'delivering our clean energy mission'. On 29 January, Rachel Reeves announced that she backed expansion of not only Heathrow but also Gatwick and Luton airports.

Reports emerged that Marco Rubio's US State Department had banned US embassies and consulates from flying flags other than the Stars and Stripes – ostensibly a response to the occasional appearance, during the Biden years, of flags supporting progressive causes, such as the rainbow colours of LGBTQ+ Pride. Trump had already, on his first day in office, shown his own colours by ordering the end of federally funded diversity, equity and inclusion programmes, and by stating that the government would recognise only two biological sexes, male and female, rejecting 'gender' identity as a meaningful category.

27 January 2025
Ella Baron
Guardian

1 February 2025
Dave Brown
Independent

The last day of January 2025 was the fifth anniversary of the UK's departure from the European Union (EU), prompting reflections on Brexit. The *Independent*'s editorial thought that 'few are dancing in the streets' about what it called 'the disaster', and the UK was proceeding 'on its path to a 4 per cent reduction in GDP' compared to where the country would have been if still inside the EU. Nigel Farage, who had pronounced Brexit 'the greatest moment in our modern history', acknowledged that the 'full benefits' had not been realised. Unsurprisingly, he suggested that only Reform UK could deliver them.

Sir Keir Starmer became the first UK prime minister since Brexit to attend a gathering of all 27 EU member states. Defence and security were on the agenda; but there was speculation about progress on a post-Brexit 'reset' given Starmer's warm relationship with EU Commission President Ursula von der Leyen. Starmer also had to nurture the 'special relationship' with a new US president who seemed to be dropping historic attachments to Europe. 'Time to bury your self-worth in full fawning mode' was John Crace's advice in the *Guardian*. In ITV's *Love Island* reality show, swimsuited couples compete for the viewers' and each other's affections.

3 February 2025
Rebecca Hendin
Guardian

5 February 2025
Guy Venables
Metro

President Trump astonished the world during a press conference with visiting Israeli prime minister Benjamin Netanyahu. The United States would, Trump said, remove Gaza's 2 million people to neighbouring Arab countries, then take it over and redevelop it mainly as a tourist resort. It would become the 'Riviera of the Middle East'. He did not think Palestinians would mind being displaced, because Gaza was a 'hellhole' and 'just a demolition site'. He had thought about this idea 'over a lot of months'. Trump first achieved wealth and fame as a property developer.

IN THE FARAGIST'S ARMS

For the first time, polls suggested that Reform UK was more popular than both the Labour and Conservative parties. There was especially bad news for the Conservatives, since the *Independent*'s poll suggested that a third of its voters in the 2024 general election had deserted to Reform. Kemi Badenoch's newly devised policy, to make it more difficult for migrants to claim 'indefinite leave to remain' in the UK, looked like an attempt to woo erstwhile Conservatives back. In Degas's painting *L'Absinthe* (1875–6), two bar-flies stare ahead disconsolately in a Paris café. Nigel Farage's fondness for pubs was well known.

8 February 2025
Dave Brown
Independent

9 February 2025
Christian Adams
Sunday Telegraph

In January 2025, the Court of Session in Edinburgh declared that the permission granted in 2023 for two new oilfields was illegal, because it did not factor in the 'downstream' impact of burning the fossil fuels produced. The decision about the future of the Jackdaw and Rosebank oilfields reverted to Ed Miliband. He had earlier called the Rosebank field 'climate vandalism', and now climate bodies such as the Grantham Institute for Climate Change warned against backing 'dirty' energy. But there was speculation that the prime minister and chancellor were pressing Miliband to give the go-ahead, to spur economic growth.

Given dire Conservative poll ratings, some Conservatives were proposing a pact with Reform UK ahead of local elections in May 2025. Kemi Badenoch rebuffed that prospect during an interview with the *Daily Telegraph* to mark her first 100 days as party leader. She thought 'the idea that you just do something with a whole different bunch of people and it's going to be fine is for the birds' and would alienate sections of the Conservatives' 'broad church'. In a YouGov poll, 58 per cent of Conservative voters either thought Farage would make a better prime minister than Badenoch or could not decide between the two.

12 February 2025
Patrick Blower
Daily Telegraph

13 February 2025
Ben Jennings
Guardian

In unusual scenes from the Oval Office of the White House, a baseball-capped Elon Musk gave a press conference on the activities of the Department of Government Efficiency. His four-year-old son was perched on his shoulders. The little boy, named X Æ A-Xii (or 'X' for short, the same as Musk's rebrand of Twitter), picked his nose and stuck his fingers in his father's ears. Donald Trump smiled passively from behind his desk and observed that 'X' had a very high IQ. Social-media memes portraying Musk as president and Trump as his subordinate had gone viral in recent weeks.

In a sharp break with the Biden years, President Trump reached out to Vladimir Putin in a 90-minute telephone call, concluding: 'I think we're on the way to getting peace.' At the same time, Trump's defense secretary said that, in effect, Russia would keep some Ukrainian territory because any return to the pre-2014 borders was 'illusionary'. The cartoon evokes David Low's 'Rendezvous' cartoon of 1939, in which Hitler and Stalin, ideological enemies, celebrate their non-aggression pact, which spelled Poland's demise. On 11 February, Trump signed an executive order banning federal bodies from buying paper straws.

14 February 2025
Dave Brown
Independent

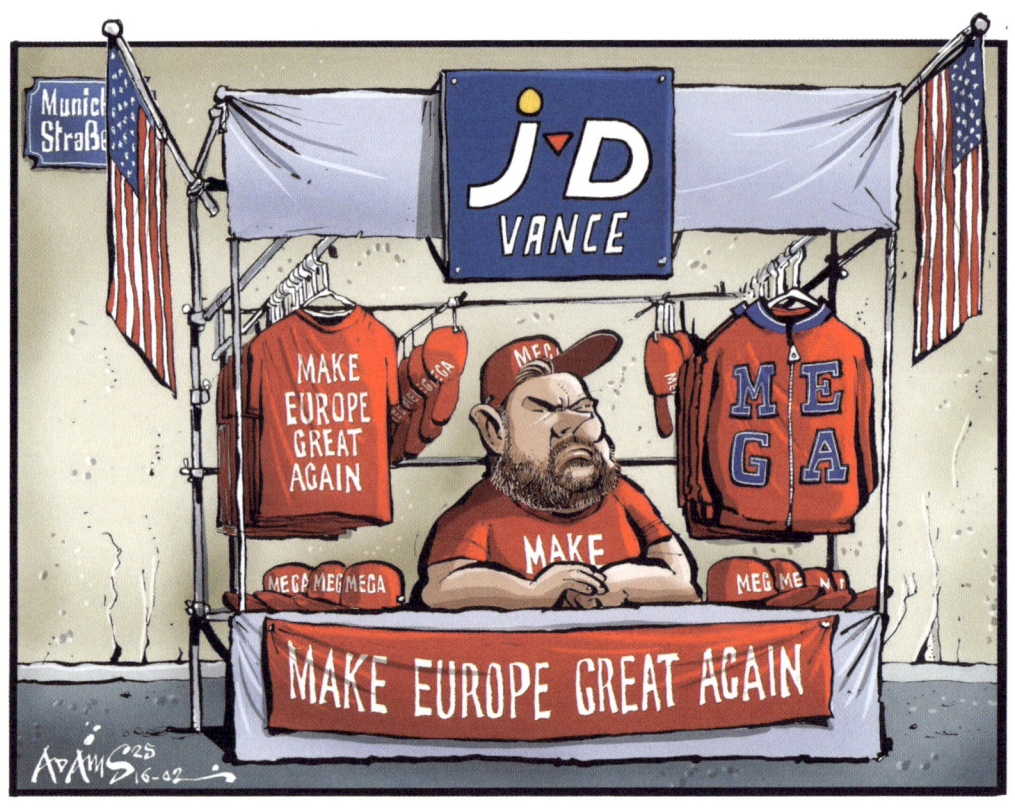

16 February 2025
Christian Adams
Sunday Telegraph

The Munich Security Conference describes itself as the 'leading forum' for 'diplomatic initiatives to address the world's most pressing security concerns'. There was nothing diplomatic about the speech given by US Vice-President JD Vance. Instead of addressing Russian threats or the war in Ukraine, he latched onto culture-war issues to criticise several European democracies, including the UK, for 'dismissing voters' concerns' on issues such as 'mass migration'. 'In Britain and across Europe, free speech, I fear, is in retreat,' he opined. As for defence, it was time, he said, for Europe to 'step up in a big way'.

After what he called his 'lengthy and very productive' call to Vladimir Putin, there was a distinct sense that President Trump prized the relationship with the Russian leader above US support for Zelensky and solidarity with Western allies like Germany's Olaf Scholz. 'I don't care so much about anything other than I want to stop having millions of people killed,' Trump said, leading some to interpret his idea of peace as Ukrainian surrender. And whereas Biden had called Putin a 'murderous dictator', Trump seemed to suggest Russia deserved some spoils of victory: 'They took a lot of land, and they fought for that land.'

17 February 2025
Nicola Jennings
Guardian

In Brussels, US Defense Secretary Pete Hegseth said that the United States was prioritising the 'security of our own borders'. In Munich, JD Vance told European leaders, including Starmer, Scholz and Macron that it was important 'for Europe to step up in a big way to provide for its own defence'. In the cartoonist's view, 'Donald Trump deserted NATO. He did a deal with Putin, excluding Zelensky, NATO and, well, Europe. Eighty years of – albeit relative – peace in Europe carelessly tossed aside by a man of no principle. Iwo Jima reminded me of America's moral high ground.' The raising of the Stars and Stripes by US Marines after the battle over Iwo Jima, in 1945, generated an iconic war photograph.

21 February 2025
Andy Davey
Daily Telegraph

On 18 February, US Secretary of State Marco Rubio met his Russian counterpart, Sergey Lavrov, in Saudi Arabia to discuss a path to peace in Ukraine. A Ukrainian delegation was not invited. Rubio reported that they had agreed to look at closer ties, better economic cooperation, and to plan a summit between Trump and Putin. 'I think I have the power to end this war,' observed Trump. In David Low's 1940 cartoon 'The Angels of Peace Descend on Belgium', three winged Nazi SS men, like vultures and led by Heinrich Himmler, float above a smoking Belgian city; Himmler carries a book entitled *Gestapo Death List*.

23 February 2025
Chris Riddell
Observer

During his first cabinet meeting, Donald Trump looked forward to signing 'a very big agreement' with President Zelensky, to recoup US money spent on Ukrainian military aid but also to make 'a lot of money in the future'. (A frequent Trumpian refrain was that Biden had foolishly squandered $300–350 billion on supporting Ukraine, though independent estimates put US support at around $120 billion.) The 'agreement' Trump meant was a deal over Ukrainian mineral resources. In fact, Ukraine had already rejected a one-sided demand to 'repay' $500 billion, and the revised agreement was to share the proceeds in a joint US–Ukrainian investment fund.

26 February 2025
Guy Venables
Metro

The warmth with which Donald Trump spoke of the authoritarian president in Russia, 'Vladimir', contrasted starkly with rhetoric used to describe the man whom he was meant to be supporting, Zelensky. On 19 February, Trump took to Truth Social to call Zelensky 'a dictator' who 'has done a terrible job' as a result of which 'MILLIONS have died'. Trump claimed that Zelensky's approval ratings were down to 4 per cent, when recent polling actually suggested 57 per cent. And Trump's allegation that Zelensky refused to hold elections omitted to mention that Ukrainian elections due in May 2022 were scuppered by Russia's invasion.

28 February 2025
Kevin Kallaugher
Economist

On 27 February, Sir Keir Starmer was in Washington, DC, to meet with President Trump. There were potentially difficult discussions ahead, on the Ukraine War, on potential US trade tariffs, and on Trump's audacious words about absorbing Canada, a Commonwealth nation, as the 51st US state. But in the Oval Office, all was charm as Starmer handed to a clearly gratified Trump a letter from King Charles, inviting him for an 'unprecedented' second state visit. During the day, Trump called both the king, and Starmer's accent, 'beautiful'. Once again, David Low's classic 'Rendezvous' (1939) was the inspiration for a cartoon.

2 March 2025
Chris Riddell
Observer

President Zelensky's White House visit on 28 February, in theory to sign the US–Ukrainian minerals deal, unravelled dramatically. A journalist's question, critiquing Zelensky for wearing his customary military-style outfit rather than a civilian suit, sparked a row in which Zelensky was verbally pummelled by Donald Trump and JD Vance. Vance accused him of ingratitude, while Trump told him he had 'no cards'. At one point, Zelensky asked Vance: 'Have you ever been to Ukraine to see the problems we have?' Vance replied: 'I've actually watched and seen the stories.' 'Great television. I will say that,' was Trump's conclusion. The deal remained unsigned.

2 March 2025
Morten Morland
Sunday Times

3 March 2025
Rebecca Hendin
Guardian

Two days after Zelensky's bruising encounter in the Oval Office, he was in London and being treated to effusive expressions of support and solidarity at an international security summit attended by European and Canadian leaders. Afterwards, Sir Keir Starmer announced the agreement of a four-point plan for Ukraine, including continued military aid, the inclusion of Ukraine in any peace talks, and ensuring Ukrainian sovereignty and defence after a peace deal. But the standout point was the Anglo-French idea to create a 'coalition of the willing' – countries that would put peacekeepers into Ukraine after a peace deal.

In late February, Sir Keir Starmer had announced the dropping of the UK's international aid budget – from 0.5 per cent of gross national income to 0.3 per cent by 2027 – in order to spend more on defence. Justifications included the Russian threat and doubts about future US commitment to European security. Although Starmer stressed that conflict itself was a big driver of poverty, the decision brought angry condemnation from charities and some MPs. The ONE campaign, a charity for Africa founded by the singer Bono, now estimated that 606,000 fewer deaths would be averted because of the aid cut.

6 March 2025
Ben Jennings
i Paper

14 March 2025
Kevin Kallaugher
Economist

As a mark of how European leaders were beginning to think the unthinkable, on 7 March the Polish prime minister, Donald Tusk, suggested that his country 'would be safer if we had our own nuclear arsenal'. For decades, most European countries had assumed they remained protected under the so-called 'nuclear umbrella' provided by the United States, and by the mutual-defence provisions of NATO. All the noises suggesting US disengagement from Europe were throwing that certainty into doubt. In France, President Macron announced 'a strategic debate on using our deterrence to protect our allies on the European continent'.

On 10 March, shares in Tesla, the electric-car company led by Elon Musk, fell by more than 15 per cent – the steepest drop in five years. Their value, which had reached nearly $480 in December 2024, had sunk to around $222; and they had fallen every week since Musk took on his government role for Donald Trump. There were reports of activists protesting at, and even vandalising, Tesla dealerships, and across the world Tesla sales were declining. On Trump's inauguration day, Musk had raised his arm exuberantly at a rally, in a gesture likened to a Nazi salute.

14 March 2025
Ben Jennings
Guardian

17 March 2025
Nicola Jennings
Guardian

In Scotland, Rachel Reeves told reporters that the welfare system was not working 'for people who need support', did not get people 'into work' and was not delivering value 'for the taxpayer'. And the bill would rise 'by billions of pounds in the next few years'. As a result, she said, 'we do need to get a grip'. Her call for 'welfare reforms' was viewed as a euphemism for cuts, since anaemic economic growth had undermined the calculations behind her October 2024 Budget. So-called personal independence payments (PIPs) looked vulnerable. The red rose is the Labour Party's logo.

On 19 March, Donald Trump reported another phone call with Vladimir Putin, describing it on his Truth Social platform as 'very good and productive'. But while Putin appeared to agree to a temporary, partial ceasefire in Ukraine, so that neither side would target the other's energy infrastructure, it seemed that Trump gained little traction on a longer, general ceasefire. Afterwards, Trump wrote that 'we will be working quickly to have a Complete Ceasefire'. By contrast, the Kremlin demanded 'the complete cessation of foreign military aid and the provision of intelligence' to Ukraine: a pre-requisite that was clearly unrealistic.

19 March 2025
Patrick Blower
Daily Telegraph

19 March 2025
Jon Davis
Guardian

As expected, on 18 March Liz Kendall, the secretary for work and pensions, announced a range of welfare changes estimated to save £5 billion. The measures to save money included moves to tighten up eligibility for personal independence payments (PIPs), paid to those with disabilities, and a halving of Universal Credit's incapacity benefit for new claimants – while removing it altogether from those aged below twenty-two. The government justified its mix of changes as an attempt to tackle 'a clear financial incentive to define yourself as incapable of work'.

For months now, opinion polls had been suggesting that while Reform UK was buoyant, the Conservatives were sinking. In launching the Conservatives' campaign for the local and mayoral elections in May 2025, Kemi Badenoch decided not to hide the grim reality: 'We're expecting this to be very challenging and, yes, that does mean losses of seats.' She added that 'July 2024 saw our worst result' in the '200 years' of the party's existence. Indeed, warming to her theme, she noted that 'if we repeated the general-election result ... we'd lose pretty much every council we're running'.

22 March 2025
Dave Brown
Independent

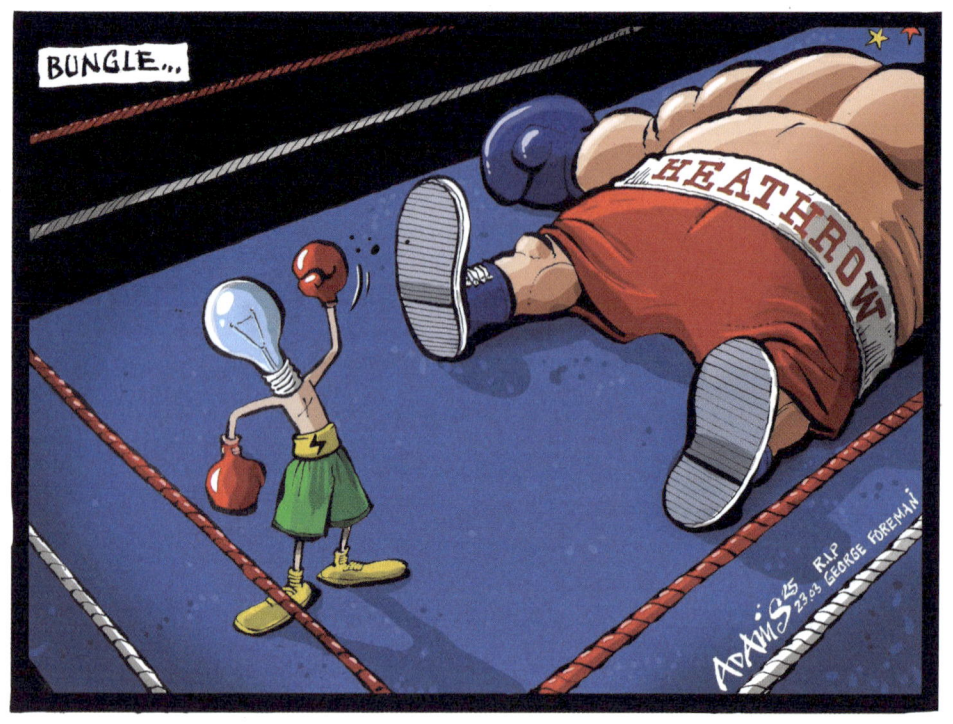

23 March 2025
Christian Adams
Sunday Telegraph

On 21 March, Heathrow airport – vital to the UK's infrastructure – suffered a power outage that forced it to close, disrupting 1,350 flights. The cause was a fire at a local electrical sub-station in Hayes, west London. Some experts suggested that an 'old transformer' filled with cooling oil had caught alight, but there was consternation at Heathrow's vulnerability. On the same day, boxing legend 'Big' George Foreman died. In 1974, he lost his world heavyweight title to Muhammad Ali in the celebrated fight dubbed the 'Rumble in the Jungle' because it took place in Zaire (Democratic Republic of Congo).

A discussion among members of Trump's administration became excruciatingly public, when the editor-in-chief of the *Atlantic* magazine was accidentally included in their Signal chat group. They spoke about an imminent US military strike on Houthi rebels in Yemen, in retaliation for attacks on shipping lanes. JD Vance resented the fact that European trade might benefit more than US trade. He told the defense secretary: 'If you think we should do it let's go. I just hate bailing Europe out again.' Hegseth agreed: 'VP: I fully share your loathing of European free-loading. It's PATHETIC.' *Hillbilly Elegy* was Vance's 2016 memoir, turned into a 2020 film.

26 March 2025
Patrick Blower
Daily Telegraph

27 March 2025
Graeme Bandeira
Northern Agenda

Rachel Reeves's Spring Statement (26 March) confirmed 'non-negotiable' cuts to the welfare bill and even extended them. The catalysts were higher debt costs, higher inflation and a revised growth forecast for the coming year, down to 1 per cent of GDP. New claimants of incapacity benefit would now also see their halved payments frozen until 2030, while the planned rise in Universal Credit was reduced by £1 per week. Reeves was determined to regain her £9.9 billion of 'fiscal headroom' to avoid breaching her fiscal rules on borrowing. Tim Burton's fantasy film *Edward Scissorhands* (1990) starred Johnny Depp.

Labour rumblings of discontent accompanied the chancellor's Spring Statement. In addition, a Department of Work and Pensions impact assessment suggested that the welfare changes would send poverty in the UK in an upwards direction. It estimated 'there will be an additional 250,000 people (including 50,000 children) in relative poverty after housing costs in 2029/30 as a result of modelled changes to social security compared to the baseline projections'. Reeves disputed that view, insisting to journalists: 'Our reforms, instead of pushing people into poverty, are going to get people into work.'

28 March 2025
Ben Jennings
Guardian

29 March 2025
Dave Brown
Independent

Ministers' freebies were back in the news when Rachel Reeves accepted tickets to see the US singer–songwriter Sabrina Carpenter at London's O2 Arena. In interview with the BBC's Laura Kuenssberg, she tried to explain that 'these weren't tickets that you could pay for'. She said: 'I do now have security which means it's not as easy as it would be in the past to just sit in a concert.' She promised to find out the gift's value for the next Register of Members' Financial Interests. The cartoonist was inspired by W. T. Smedley (1858–1920), an American magazine illustrator.

Against the background of Donald Trump's assertion that the United States should take over Greenland, Vice-President Vance accompanied his wife, Usha, on a brief trip to the autonomous Danish territory. Originally billed as a visit by just the US second lady, it was rearranged and shortened because local people refused invitations to speak with her and local businesses did not want to engage. In the end, the couple visited the isolated US missile-defence base at Pituffik, where the vice-president said Denmark 'had not done a good job' for Greenlanders. Meanwhile, Donald Trump still insisted: 'We have to have Greenland.'

29 March 2025
Ben Jennings
i Paper

On 2 April, President Trump held a press conference to announce 'Liberation Day': global tariffs to be imposed on most goods imported into the United States. While imports from Britain faced the baseline 10 per cent tariff, the EU suffered a rate of 20 per cent; and steel imports were charged at 25 per cent. Imports from some small countries with big trade imbalances with the United States received tariffs as high as 50 per cent. The US tariffs were described as its biggest since the Second World War – a time when the United States had aided Europe in a very different sort of liberation.

2 April 2025
Patrick Blower
Daily Telegraph

Donald Trump told reporters he thought Sir Keir Starmer was 'very happy about how we treated' the UK on tariffs, even though an estimated £175 billion had been wiped off the value of UK shares and pension funds in a matter of days. While a number of nations and trading blocs, such as China and the European Union, were drawing up reciprocal tariffs on imports from the United States, the British government held back from countermeasures, preferring the twin strategy of trying to negotiate a trade deal and emphasising the soft diplomacy of the second state visit offered to Trump.

6 April 2025
Chris Riddell
Observer

7 April 2025
Patrick Blower
Daily Telegraph

Rubbish continued to pile up in the streets of Birmingham as a result of a strike by members of the Unite union: they opposed the City Council's plans for pay reform and role changes in the waste service. On 31 March, the city authorities declared a 'major incident', admitting that 'around 17,000 tonnes of waste remains uncollected across the city', with daily accumulations put at 900 tonnes. Picket lines were blocking depots, so that only a fraction of the 200 refuse lorries were in action. In October 2023, faced with settling an expensive equal-pay award, Birmingham had effectively declared itself bankrupt.

There was speculation that Sir Keir Starmer might wobble over the UK's ban on US chlorine-washed chicken and hormone-treated beef in order to win a trade deal from Donald Trump. In a 'factsheet' accompanying the 10 per cent tariff on imports from Britain, the White House took aim at what it called the UK's 'non-science-based standards' and defended its own beef and poultry as 'high-quality' – even though chlorination was a response to the high levels of salmonella and other bacteria found in US poultry farming. There was little evidence that British consumers or farmers had an appetite to dilute UK food standards.

8 April 2025
Ben Jennings
Guardian

11 April 2025
Kevin Kallaugher
Economist

By far the biggest US import tariffs were those imposed on Chinese goods. By 9 April, they had reached 104 per cent. 'BE COOL!' President Trump tried to reassure Americans faced with higher prices and stock-market uncertainty, 'Everything is going to work out well,' while also urging US companies to relocate production away from China, back to the United States. An unbowed China responded by raising its own tariffs on US imports to 84 per cent, declaring it would 'never sit idly by' and let 'the Chinese people be damaged and deprived'.

On 10 April, President Trump suddenly announced a 90-day pause in import tariffs above 10 per cent for most countries, just as they were coming into effect. The *Guardian* called it a 'shock retreat'. Trump's defenders portrayed the unpredictability as a purposeful policy to bring trading partners to the negotiating table; but many commentators put the reversal down to the shocks felt by the US stock market and the US bond market, which had seen the price of US borrowing soar. Despite an immediate bounce back, US share prices remained lower than they had been before 'Liberation Day'.

11 April 2025
Ben Jennings
Guardian

Sir Keir Starmer dramatically interrupted MPs' Easter holidays to recall parliament on Saturday 12 April. The reason was to pass emergency legislation bypassing the Chinese Jingye Group, owners of British Steel, to deliver the raw materials needed by its Scunthorpe plant and keep the blast furnaces there operating – the only UK furnaces still capable of producing primary (structural) steel. The move to take control was framed as a strategic necessity, but not *yet* quite a nationalisation. 'Is it a bird? Is it a plane? No, it's Superman!' is a slogan attributed to DC Comics' tales of the superhero.

13 April 2025
Christian Adams
Sunday Telegraph

The volatility in international markets brought on by President Trump's on-again, off-again tariffs gave the appearance of policy made almost on a daily whim. While the 'reciprocal' US import tariffs had been suspended with respect to many nations, the trade war with China only intensified, as total US tariffs on imports from China reached an eye-watering 145 per cent. For different reasons, the remote Heard Island and McDonald Islands, in the Indian Ocean, attracted attention after they were subjected to a tariff rate of 10 per cent. The islands have no human inhabitants, but a sizeable population of penguins and seals.

17 April 2025
Kevin Kallaugher
Economist

17 April 2025
Patrick Blower
Daily Telegraph

For several years, J. K. Rowling, author of the Harry Potter books, had been intervening in the heated debate on sex and gender, advancing the view that some legislation on transgender rights undermined the rights of women and girls. On 16 April, a long-running battle about the scope of the Scottish Equality Act (2010) ended with the UK Supreme Court's decision that definitions of 'sex', 'man' and 'woman' referred to biological sex ('a person's sex at birth') and could not encompass a change of gender obtained with a Gender Recognition Certificate. Rowling praised the verdict, which was likely to have widespread implications.

In 2024, the United States had exported $11.9 billion more in goods to the UK than the UK exported to the United States. Despite enjoying that trade surplus, Donald Trump's administration still subjected the UK to its baseline 10 per cent import tariff, with higher levels for steel and cars. Nevertheless, unlike Canada, China and the EU, Sir Keir Starmer was among the few national leaders not to introduce retaliatory tariffs, earning praise from some and scorn for weakness from others. At the White House, JD Vance suggested there was a 'good chance' of a trade deal – but at what price?

17 April 2025
Dave Brown
Independent

18 April 2025
Andy Davey
Daily Telegraph

The IMF [International Monetary Fund] announced that we are all younger than previous generations; for the current boomers that means '70 is the new 50' and that they should carry on working. At the same time, Sir Keir Starmer announced that he would slash the NHS waiting list by encouraging GPs to refer patients to outside specialists, rather than adding to the endless list of people waiting for a hospital specialist. In April, the government announced an expansion of its scheme paying GP practices £20 for every patient with lesser ailments that they managed to divert from hospital referrals.

On 18 April, Vladimir Putin announced a 30-hour truce in hostilities against Ukraine – a modest peace offering for Easter, falling short of the 30-day ceasefire that Ukraine and the United States wanted. Volodymyr Zelensky called it a fraudulent exercise in 'PR', and the British government called it a 'stunt'. By the time it terminated on 20 April, Ukraine alleged more than 1,800 breaches by Russia, while Russia fired back counterclaims of Ukrainian actions. Donald Trump suggested that the United States might 'take a pass' on brokering peace and again implied that both belligerents were equally responsible for the war.

21 April 2025
Ella Baron
Guardian

22 April 2025
Rebecca Hendin
Guardian

The frail Pope Francis died at his residence in the Vatican City on 21 April, having met JD Vance just the day before. Donald Trump proclaimed: 'Rest in Peace Pope Francis!' before confirming that he and Melania would attend the funeral in Rome. Earlier that day, Trump had taken to Truth Social to lambast the chair of the US Federal Reserve as a 'major loser' for not lowering US interest rates. In the days following, Trump joked with reporters that he'd 'like to be pope' and posted an AI image of himself in pontifical robes; it was shared by the White House.

On 22 April, Rachel Reeves flew into Washington, DC, to lobby for a trade deal that would offer some UK concessions – such as a reduction in the 'digital tax' affecting major US companies – in return for a lowering of the steep US import tariffs on steel, cars and aluminium. The mood was upbeat, with British government sources indicating that a signature-ready deal was available. But the next day, the *Wall Street Journal* leaked a document suggesting that the Trump administration wanted further concessions, including in agriculture. *Trump: The Art of the Deal* (1987) was the US president's ghostwritten business memoir. In regard to this cartoon, someone on social media wrote: 'It's rather unfortunate in this context that the cartoonist's name is Blower!'

23 April 2025
Patrick Blower
Daily Telegraph

Relations between the Trump administration and President Zelensky became prickly once more, as it became clearer that that US proposals for peace in Ukraine required the country to cede Crimea, and possibly other territories, too, to Russia. While Zelensky praised the collective efforts of European leaders, and evoked earlier US condemnations of the seizure of Crimea, Trump declared Zelensky's comments 'harmful' and 'inflammatory'. The US president again called Zelensky 'the man with "no cards to play"', portraying him as someone perpetuating the 'killing field'.

25 April 2025
Kevin Kallaugher
Economist

The *Daily Telegraph* suggested that, under plans for 'zonal pricing', inhabitants of southern England could end up paying more for their electricity than users elsewhere in the UK. In this 'biggest shake-up since privatisation', areas more reliant on (cheaper) wind and solar power would have lower bills than areas more reliant on fossil fuels. Amid a short-lived, but heated, flurry of media comment and debate, Energy Security and Climate Change Secretary Ed Miliband acknowledged that reforms were being considered; but he insisted he was 'not going to take a decision that is going to raise prices in some parts of the country'.

26 April 2025
Dave Brown
Independent

29 April 2025
Peter Schrank
The Times

On 28 April, Canadians voted in a snap general election called by the Liberal Party leader and prime minister, Mark Carney. Until his predecessor, Justin Trudeau, had stood down, the Liberals had trailed the opposition Conservatives badly in opinion polls. But the election of Donald Trump, followed by the US import tariffs and rhetoric about Canada as the '51st US state', had stirred Canadian patriotism and boosted support for Carney's robust responses to Trump. The Liberals held onto power. The cartoonist described this as 'a simple and straightforward image. And Trump isn't in it. He's getting too much attention already.'

The biggest winners from local and mayoral elections (1 May) were Nigel Farage's Reform UK. From a base of around 100 councillors, Reform gained another 677, snatching control of eight councils from the Conservatives – who lost 674 councillors and all the councils they were defending. Kemi Badenoch called it a 'bloodbath'. Labour had fewer authorities to defend but shed 187 councillors and lost, by six votes, the parliamentary seat of Runcorn and Helsby to Reform. Candidates gazing into unfixed potholes is a staple of municipal politics, while in Greek mythology, Narcissus fell in love with his own reflection in a pool of water.

3 May 2025
Ben Jennings
Guardian

President Trump declared that films made outside the United States, with foreign tax breaks, constituted a 'National Security threat' and foreign 'messaging and propaganda'. 'WE WANT MOVIES MADE IN AMERICA, AGAIN!' he proclaimed on Truth Social, to avoid a 'very fast death' of Hollywood. He wanted a tariff of 100 per cent on films made abroad. Given the complexity of the way films are funded, produced and disseminated, with Hollywood frequently choosing facilities and settings abroad, there was immediate confusion as to the implications. Francis Ford Coppola's movie *Apocalypse Now* (1979) tackled the Vietnam War.

6 May 2025
Patrick Blower
Daily Telegraph

On 6 May, shortly after his election success, Canadian Prime Minister Mark Carney sat in the Oval Office opposite the man who had, arguably, and inadvertently, delivered his victory: Donald Trump. The atmosphere was awkwardly courteous. Dropping the dismissive references to the Canadian prime minister as a provincial 'governor', Trump said he wanted 'to be friends with Canada'. Carney suggested to Trump: 'As you know from real estate, there are some places that are never for sale', and his voters had demonstrated that Canada 'won't be for sale, ever'. 'Never say never,' suggested Trump, as Carney whispered 'never'.

9 May 2025
Kevin Kallaugher
Economist

9 May 2025
Andy Davey
Daily Telegraph

Following the Labour losses in the 1 May local elections, there were rumblings of backbench rebellion. The Labour first minister of Wales, Lady (Eluned) Morgan, broke ranks to call on the Westminster government to reinstate the winter fuel payment, suggesting that its withdrawal from millions of pensioners was alienating voters. Sir Keir Starmer insisted he was listening; and he denied he was consoling himself in the 'warm bath' of dismissing Labour's unpopularity as inevitable at this point in the 'electoral cycle'; but he did not suggest a change of direction, and his press secretary insisted he would not be 'blown off course'.

Home Secretary Yvette Cooper told the BBC's Laura Kuenssberg that Labour would 'end care worker recruitment from abroad', although existing foreign workers would be able to extend their visas. The government billed the measures, elaborated in a White Paper, as an effort to 'restore order, control and fairness to the system, bring down net migration and promote economic growth'. Henceforth, Cooper said, care providers would need to recruit more 'British nationals'. In a BBC projection, based on the 1 May voting, Reform UK would capture 30 per cent of votes in a general election, compared to Labour's 20 per cent.

11 May 2025
Andy Bunday
Sunday Mirror

Vladimir Putin was unimpressed by the ultimatum delivered to him by European leaders after they convened in Kiev: agree to an unconditional 30-day ceasefire with Ukraine or face further sanctions. Sir Keir Starmer said it was Putin's chance to show he was 'serious' about peace. Putin dismissed the leaders' 'boorish manner' and offered direct discussion with Ukraine, in Turkey, but without lifting hostilities. President Trump thought the offer was 'potentially great', while analysts suggested that Putin's strategy was to widen the emerging differences between the United States and Europe over the Ukraine War.

12 May 2025
Nicola Jennings
Guardian

Sir Keir Starmer told the press that the Immigration White Paper 'will finally take back control of our borders and close the book on a squalid chapter for our politics, our economy, and our country'. He also suggested that if immigrants did not integrate and follow shared rules, Britain could become an 'island of strangers'. Some senior Labour figures disassociated themselves from his language; to some, it evoked Enoch Powell's references to white people 'made strangers in their own country' in his notorious 'Rivers of Blood' speech (1968). Starmer rejected the comparisons, pleading the wider context of his speech.

15 May 2025
Dave Brown
Independent

17 May 2025
Ben Jennings
Guardian

For the first time in three years, Russian and Ukrainian delegations met to discuss a possible ceasefire, in talks hosted by Turkey. The low expectations of a breakthrough proved correct. Although Vladimir Medinsky, leader of the Russian delegation, thought it had gone well, he rejected an immediate 30-day ceasefire. Instead, his team pressed for further discussions and a set of conditions that were inevitably unacceptable to Ukraine, including Ukrainian withdrawals from eastern Ukrainian provinces that Russia was fighting to control. Zelensky dismissed the meeting as 'low level', and Sir Keir Starmer called the Russian position 'clearly unacceptable'.

Sir Keir Starmer hailed a 'reset' in UK–EU relations after signing a wide-ranging deal that, he said, 'gives us unprecedented access to EU markets'. A similarly enthusiastic Ursula von der Leyen applauded 'a new chapter in our relationship'. The agreement paved the way for the smoother and easier passage of goods and people, but Brexit backers accused Starmer of making the UK 'rule takers' again. On 17 May, the British entry in the Eurovision Song Contest – 'What the Hell Just Happened?' by the trio Remember Monday – crashed out when it received a shock *nul points* from the voting public.

19 May 2025
Steve Bright
Sun

20 May 2025
Morten Morland
The Times

When the UK–EU deal was announced, Conservatives and Reform UK politicians attacked it. Kemi Badenoch called the meeting at London's Lancaster House a 'surrender summit' and promised to reverse the agreement 'at the first opportunity'. The concession allowing EU fishermen another 12 years of access to British waters – in exchange for British exports of seafood to the EU – was a major bone of contention. Nigel Farage deplored the role of the European Court of Justice in brokering disputes, too, accusing Starmer of 'making the UK subject to a foreign court once more' as well as the 'overt assassination of our fishing industry'.

President Trump announced agreement on a design for the so-called 'Golden Dome': a missile-defence shield to counter the most advanced weapons that might be launched at the United States. The programme, priced at $175 billion, was ambitious, not least because Trump declared it would be ready within four years. According to the cartoonist, 'I was reluctant to do this one. I thought it was a day to focus on the horrors of Gaza . . . Still, it was fun to do something about Trump's increasingly ludicrous comb-over. He must spend more time primping his hair than he does informing himself about world affairs.'

22 May 2025
Peter Schrank
The Times

23 May 2025
Dave Brown
Independent

There was mounting pressure – from within and without the Labour Party, and from the punishing local election results – for the government to reverse course on limiting the winter fuel payment to the 1.5 million pensioners claiming pension credit. For months, Sir Keir Starmer and Rachel Reeves had insisted they would not be diverted from the policy. But on 21 May, Starmer claimed at Prime Minister's Questions that a better-than-anticipated economic outlook meant he could look at making more pensioners eligible for the payment. Although there was no detail, his words were immediately interpreted as a reluctant U-turn.

Israel's latest actions in Gaza stretched even traditional allies beyond endurance. In the wake of a new Israeli ground offensive called 'Operation Gideon's Chariot', Britain, France and Canada issued a joint statement. They condemned Israel's 'egregious actions' and the 'intolerable' suffering caused by Israel's blockade of humanitarian aid for more than 11 weeks. At the same time, the United Nations warned that thousands of Palestinian babies were at risk of death within days. In the House of Commons, Foreign Secretary David Lammy castigated Israel's actions as 'indefensible', warning that 'the world is judging, history will judge them.'

23 May 2025
Kevin Kallaugher
Economist

Finally, the UK signed an agreement to hand sovereignty of the Chagos Islands to Mauritius, along with £1.25 billion in development funds over 25 years. For an annual fee of £120 million (plus inflation), the UK would get a 99-year lease on the Diego Garcia military base, used by UK and US forces. Labour ministers insisted that, without a deal, further international legal action would undermine the utility of the base. The Mauritian prime minister welcomed the deal as one of the last chapters of decolonisation; in Britain, critics attacked the £30 billion total price tag and warned of potential Chinese influence over Mauritius.

24 May 2025
Christian Adams
Daily Telegraph

Donald Trump's reluctance to criticise Vladimir Putin or Russia, especially when contrasted with his readiness to berate Volodymyr Zelensky and Ukraine, was becoming a pervading if perplexing theme of his second presidency. And, clearly, Putin preferred Trump to Biden. But after Russia launched its largest aerial attack yet on Ukraine, on 24–25 May, an impatient Trump let loose on Truth Social. In response, Putin's spokesman said: 'This is a very crucial moment, which is naturally accompanied by emotional overload on all sides and emotional reactions.'

27 May 2025
Ella Baron
Guardian

Nigel Farage announced that Reform UK, if elected to power, would scrap Labour's restriction of means-tested child-related benefits to a family's first two children (if subsequent children were born after 2017). The twice-divorced Farage said he wanted to encourage marriage by doubling a married partner's tax threshold to £25,000. Promising to cut 'net immigration to zero', Reform would also 'do everything in its power to encourage British people who are able and want kids to have them'. Farage admitted that the plans were 'expensive', as critics from across the political spectrum attacked him for unfunded tax cuts and spending splurges.

29 May 2025
Nicola Jennings
Guardian

The acronym TACO – 'Trump Always Chickens Out' – was coined by a *Financial Times* columnist and used as a shorthand by some on Wall Street to indicate that traders should not fret too much about Trump's regular threat of tariffs against other countries, since he usually backed down. When asked about the acronym by a CNBC reporter, Trump lashed out, saying 'I've never heard that', before defending his approach: 'it's called negotiation'. Chris Riddell's cartoon also manages to squeeze in references to one of Trump's favourite meals (a Big Mac), his erstwhile ally Elon Musk, Musk's cost-cutting work at the Department of Government Efficiency (DOGE), and his infamous hand gesture at an Inauguration Day rally that was widely interpreted as a Nazi salute.

1 June 2025
Chris Riddell
Observer

On 2 June the government released a defence review that concluded that the UK faced a 'new era of threat', owing to the 'immediate and pressing' danger posed by Russia and other countries, including China. Defence Secretary John Healey championed the government's proposed response, arguing: 'This is Britain standing behind making our Armed Forces stronger but making our industrial base stronger, and this is part of our readiness to fight if required.' For the cartoonist, the famous 'Don't Panic!' catchphrase from the BBC sitcom *Dad's Army* 'seemed to blend nicely with the idea of the British lion as an ineffectual and lazy old peacenik'.

2 June 2025
Peter Schrank
The Times

In the course of meetings held in Istanbul between Russian and Ukrainian negotiators, Russia rejected Kyiv's call for a month-long unconditional ceasefire, and instead presented a 'memorandum' of terms for the cessation of hostilities. These included the demands that Ukraine must cede large swathes of territory and accept limits on its military capability. According to a Ukrainian representative, the 'Russian side passed a set of old ultimatums that do not move the situation any closer to true peace.'

3 June 2025
Morten Morland
The Times

Elon Musk was vocal in his opposition to the 'One Big Beautiful Bill Act', passed by Congress on 22 May. In an interview with CBS, he said: 'I think a bill can be big or it could be beautiful. But I don't know if it could be both.' Posting on X on 4 June he described the bill as a 'disgusting abomination' and urged people to 'Call your Senator, Call your Congressman', adding that 'Bankrupting America is NOT ok!'. Shortly after Musk's post, the White House released a statement asserting that 'by every honest metric, President Donald J. Trump's One Big Beautiful Bill dramatically improves the fiscal trajectory of the United States and unleashes an era of unprecedented economic growth.' Elon Musk had left the Trump administration at the end of May after 130 days, a day after his initial criticism of the budget bill.

6 June 2025
Kevin Kallaugher
Economist

After Musk's initial criticism of Trump's spending bill, the rest of the world was treated to the unedifying spectacle of the two men's feud playing out in full view on their respective social media platforms: X and Truth Social. Musk accused Trump of 'such ingratitude', and posted on X that 'without me, Trump would have lost the election', before floating the need to create a new political party. When Trump threatened to cut Musk's government contracts, Musk responded by calling for Trump's impeachment. At the Oval Office on 5 June Trump stated that he was 'very surprised' and 'disappointed' by Musk's criticisms. 'Elon and I had a great relationship,' he said. 'I don't know if we will anymore.' By 7 June Musk had deleted several of his posts.

7 June 2025
Christian Adams
Daily Telegraph

10 June 2025
Patrick Blower
Daily Telegraph

As the Israel–Hamas conflict entered its 20th month, the *Madleen*, a UK-flagged vessel seeking both to draw international attention to the crisis and to deliver aid to the stricken Gaza Strip, was seized by the Israeli military in international waters. The twelve crew members included the *Game of Thrones* actor Liam Cunningham, Rima Hassan (a French member of the European Parliament) and also Swedish activist Greta Thunberg, whose detractors queried why someone best known for her campaigns to reverse climate change would now be focussing on a conflict in the Middle East.

On 10 June the government announced that it planned to invest £14.2 billion in a new nuclear power station on the Suffolk coast, known as Sizewell C. Critics worried about the development's cost and environmental impact, but Keir Starmer argued that it would usher in 'lower energy bills, thousands more jobs and apprenticeships, and better energy security' and that it was 'a vote of confidence in the UK as an investment destination'. His statement came just one day before Chancellor Rachel Reeves was expected to announce significant welfare cuts in her June spending review.

11 June 2025
Seamus Jennings
The Times

12 June 2025
Ben Jennings
Guardian

Following the very public falling out between Elon Musk and Donald Trump over Trump's 'One Big Beautiful Bill', there were reports that Musk had called the president to express remorse for some of the things he had said about him on X. According to Trump there were 'no hard feelings'. 'I think he feels very badly that he said that,' he said of his erstwhile ally's blistering social media barrage.

One day after the 11 June spending review had set out government plans for boosting growth (while simultaneously increasing NHS and defence spending), the latest GDP figures revealed that, in April, the economy had actually shrunk by 0.3 per cent, its worst monthly contraction for 18 months. Higher taxes for businesses, Trump's tariffs and stamp duty changes were identified as some of the culprits. According to the cartoonist, the chancellor had 'set her sights on growth as her salvation in the spending review, but the next morning, as if nobody had checked the diary, the ONS [Office for National Statistics] reported that growth had headed in the anti-growth direction.'

13 June 2025
Andy Davey
Daily Telegraph

15 June 2025
Christian Adams
Sunday Telegraph

Israel's surprise missile attacks on the Islamic Republic of Iran on 13 June resulted in the deaths of many of Iran's top military personnel and senior nuclear scientists, and caused substantial degradation of its military capabilities. The country's nuclear facilities, which had earned the country nearly two decades of US and international sanctions, were also significantly damaged. While Tehran responded to the attacks by launching missiles at Israel (most of which were intercepted), Iranian moderates voiced criticism of 86-year-old Ayatollah Ali Khamenei, the country's supreme leader since 1989, blaming him for the country's predicament, and questioning his ideological goals and nuclear ambitions.

With tensions in the Middle East increasing as the conflict between Israel and Iran escalated, demonstrators took to the streets worldwide to protest against the bombing of the Islamic Republic. Some commentators criticised the protestors, arguing that they failed to acknowledge that they enjoyed a social liberalism and freedom to demonstrate in the West that would not be afforded to them by the repressive regime of the country that they sought to defend: Iran.

16 June 2025
Patrick Blower
Daily Telegraph

Under pressure following several policy U-turns since taking office, Sir Keir Starmer was accused of yet another when, having initially resisted calls for a full public inquiry into child grooming gangs, he announced on 14 June that he would be now be authorising one. His decision, which followed months of pressure from opposition parties, and which was viewed by the likes of Nigel Farage and Kemi Badenoch as a significant volte-face, was a response to the recommendations of an independent report by Baroness (Louise) Casey. Previously Starmer had argued that the government would focus on putting in place the recommendations made in Professor Alexis Jay's 2022 report on child sexual abuse. Other U-turns laid at the prime minister's door included those on international aid, national insurance payments, the winter fuel allowance, benefits cuts and policies towards trans women.

16 June 2025
Steve Bright
Sun

With Israel requesting American support for its military action against Iran, Sir Keir Starmer urged President Donald Trump to focus instead on 'de-escalation', arguing that US military involvement could have damaging regional and global repercussions. At the G7 summit in Canada, Starmer seemed confident that Trump would not authorise an attack: 'There is nothing the president said that suggests he's about to get involved in this conflict,' he stated. Trump himself said that he would decide on a course of action over the following two weeks, and criticised the *Wall Street Journal* for suggesting that he had privately approved attack plans (the journal had 'No Idea what my thoughts are concerning Iran!' he stated in a message he posted on Truth Social).

21 June 2025
Ben Jennings
Guardian

Just over a week after Israel's surprise attack on Iran, and amid considerable international speculation, the US became actively involved in the conflict when President Trump authorised air strikes on three Iranian nuclear sites. In a televised address Trump described the strikes as a 'spectacular military success' and demanded that 'Iran, the bully of the Middle East, must now make peace.' While Trump seemed hopeful that the strikes would compel Iran to return to negotiations, others raised concerns that the action could open a 'Pandora's Box' of unforeseen and very dangerous consequences.

24 June 2025
Guy Venables
Metro

With changes in the tax regime on the political agenda for those not permanently domiciled in the UK, and fears of an ensuing exodus of high-net-worth individuals, Reform UK proposed a plan whereby 'non-doms' could bypass some UK taxes by paying a flat £250,000 fee. In return they would receive a Britannia Card, allowing them to avoid taxes on foreign wealth, income and capital gains, as well as inheritance tax. The income raised, Nigel Farage claimed, would be distributed to the lowest-paid workers. Reform estimated that this 'Robin Hood' tax could generate £1.5 billion to £2.5 billion annually, benefiting low-paid workers by somewhere between £600 and £1,000 each. Chancellor of the Exchequer Rachel Reeves, however, criticised the plan as a 'tax cut for foreign billionaires'.

24 June 2025
Patrick Blower
Daily Telegraph

27 June 2025
Morten Morland
The Times

The government's flagship welfare reform bill was due to be voted on in Parliament on 1 July. However, a potential rebellion by 120 backbenchers, who were unhappy with the planned cuts to social security payments it entailed, prompted concessions that threatened to add up to £3 billion a year to an already vast £40 billion black hole that Chancellor of the Exchequer Rachel Reeves wanted to fill at the next Budget. The embarrassing U-turn she and the prime minister were obliged to make prompted political commentators to say that the pair were out of step with, and insufficiently engaged with, Labour MPs.

Organisers of the Glastonbury Festival found themselves embroiled in controversy, first over hosting the pro-Palestinian Irish band Kneecap, and then over rap-punk duo Bob Vylan's onstage denunciation of the Israel Defence Forces (IDF). The organisers said the festival 'does not condone hate speech or incitement to violence of any kind from its performers'. For their part, Bob Vylan, who had led the crowd in the chant 'Death, death to the IDF', subsequently stated: 'We are not for the death of Jews, Arabs or any other race or group of people.' Here, Patrick Blower compares elements of the Glastonbury Festival of 2025 with the famous counterculture Summer of Love of 1967.

30 June 2025
Patrick Blower
Daily Telegraph

Despite previous concessions to disgruntled and restive Labour MPs, the government performed yet another U-turn on the welfare reform bill – more properly, the 'Universal Credit and Personal Independence Payment Bill' – to avert potential defeat at the second reading. Barely two hours before MPs voted, it was agreed that the rules surrounding PIP would not be reformed ahead of the review into the possible ramifications. The government won the vote, but with its parliamentary majority more than halved to 75 votes. The combination of rebellion and U-turn left Sir Keir Starmer bloodied, his authority undermined.

3 July 2025
Dave Brown
Independent

On 4 July – US Independence Day – President Trump signed his 'One Big Beautiful Bill' into law. The White House newsletter boasted of the 'largest tax cut in history', 'bigger paychecks' and the 'expansion of domestic oil and gas production', as well as more spending on, for example, 'Border Patrol agents' and the futuristic Gold Dome missile shield. 'The people are happy!' proclaimed Trump. However, the bill, which very narrowly passed through Congress, appalled some fiscal conservatives, while Democrats saw it as an assault on healthcare provision and a tax gift for the wealthy.

4 July 2025
Ben Jennings
Guardian

5 July 2025
Peter Brookes
The Times

On 3 July, Zarah Sultana, MP for Coventry South, announced that she was leaving the Labour Party – from which she was already suspended – to join Jeremy Corbyn's Independent Alliance. Not only that, she declared she would 'co-lead' a new left-of-centre political party that Corbyn had been nurturing, but whose details remained vague. The next day, the band Oasis, fronted by the fractious Gallagher brothers and whose album *Definitely Maybe* topped the charts in 1994, began their comeback 'Live '25 Tour' with a concert in Cardiff. A week earlier, the grizzled rocker Neil Young had played the 'Legends' slot at the Glastonbury Festival.

Economists suggested that the government's U-turns over the welfare reform bill had effectively wiped out the savings of around £4.5 billion that the bill was intended to deliver. The next day, at Prime Minister's Questions, Sir Keir Starmer side-stepped interrogation about Rachel Reeves's future, but notably did not confirm that she would remain as chancellor. Behind him sat a visibly upset Reeves, wiping away tears. She later said that she was dealing with an undisclosed personal matter, but the scene compounded the sense of a government in trouble, causing jitters in the financial markets, as the pound fell.

6 July 2025
Christian Adams
Sunday Telegraph

10 July 2025
Dave Brown
Independent

President Macron arrived in the UK on a state visit as it was being trailed that Sir Keir Starmer wanted a 'one in, one out' arrangement for 'irregular' migrants arriving on small boats from the French coast. On 10 July, the leaders announced the plan, which Starmer called an 'experiment': for every small boat arrival sent back to France, the UK would take, and process through a new route, a migrant who had not previously attempted to cross the Channel. They also reached agreement on allowing the 11th-century Bayeux Tapestry to travel to Britain for the first time. It depicts the Norman conquest of England in 1066, when a different sort of Channel crossing changed history.

On 3 July, Parliament voted through amendments to the 2000 Terrorist Act, which officially proscribed the direct-action protest group Palestine Action, alongside two right-wing, white supremacist groups. The catalyst for Palestine Action's inclusion was a break-in at RAF Brize Norton, and the spray-painting of two aircraft, by the group's activists. Palestine Action rejected the 'terrorist' tag, asserting that its legitimate 'civil disobedience' campaign had been crudely 'bundled in with two violent, neo-Nazi militias'. By 12 July, more than 70 people had been arrested for protesting in defence of the group. Among those detained was an 83-year-old retired priest. Despite the uproar over her arrest, the head of the Metropolitan Police said the law did 'not have an age limit'.

14 July 2025
Ella Barron
Guardian

The Labour government announced it would bring forward plans to reduce the voting age to 16, by passing the legislation before the next general election. With Reform UK riding high in the polls, critics suggested that Labour was being panicked into the move because younger people were more likely to vote for left-of-centre and progressive parties. The Liberal Democrats supported the move, while electoral guru Sir John Curtice suggested the Green Party might be the main beneficiary. For the cartoonist, 'Starmer chased the "yoof" vote . . . He's down wiv da kids y'know. But will it backfire? Will Farage schmooze them with empty promises?'

18 July 2025
Andy Davey
Daily Telegraph

Ahead of Parliament's summer recess, the prime minister sought to reassert his authority over his party in the wake of rebellions and government climbdowns. Despite all the concessions over the welfare reform bill, 47 Labour MPs had still rebelled on its final reading. Now, four prominent Labour rebels and government critics lost the Labour whip. An emboldened Starmer insisted he 'had to deal with people who repeatedly break the whip' if Labour was to 'carry through' its measures to 'change this country for the better'. Another three Labour MPs found themselves ejected from their roles as trade envoys for failing to toe the line.

18 July 2025
Ben Jennings
Guardian

On 17 July, one veteran Labour MP found herself whip-less, again. In 2023, Diane Abbott – who had been shadow home secretary during Jeremy Corbyn's leadership – was suspended from the Parliamentary Labour Party for her suggestion that antisemitism was not racism but rather 'prejudice'. The row came back to haunt her now, after she defended her view that racism was about skin-colour – although she insisted she had fought against antisemitism all her life. The cartoonist was inspired by French artist Jean-Paul Laurens, who painted *L'Interrogatoire* in 1881/2, evoking the literally torturous interrogation of a heretical monk at the hands of papal inquisitors.

19 July 2025
Dave Brown
Independent

Donald Trump appeared to be on the defensive against his MAGA base, by failing to live up to his pre-election promise to release all known information about the convicted paedophile and sex-trafficker Jeffrey Epstein. Epstein, who had cultivated the rich and influential, committed suicide in prison during Trump's first presidency; but his crimes fed conspiracy theories about a deep-state elite pulling the strings of power while indulging their depraved appetites. The *Wall Street Journal* was now alleging that Trump had sent Epstein a licentious birthday card in 2003, while other newspapers suggested that Trump had learned he was mentioned in the so-called, unreleased 'Epstein Files'.

20 July 2025
Chris Riddell
Observer

On 20 July, Environment Secretary Steve Reed announced his 'pledge' to clean up Britain's waterways and coastlines: 'The Government will halve sewage pollution from water companies by the end of the decade.' More specifically, the plan was to halve the spillage from storm overflows – in 2024 there were 32 discharges per storm – as well as halve the levels of phosphorus, to reduce the proliferation of damaging algae. The investment needed would be £104 billion. Reed tried to reassure consumers they would 'never again' see massive hikes in water bills, as had occurred in April 2025, after years of under-investment.

21 July 2025
Pete Songi
Guardian

Several large protests – sometimes with violence against police – had taken place in July outside the Bell Hotel in Epping, Essex, with the aim of expelling its asylum-seeker residents. The spark was news that one of the asylum seekers had been charged with sexual assault and harassment of a girl. The cartoonist commented: 'The *Times* online gives readers the opportunity to comment on cartoons. I try to stay away from it, but I did check out the comments for this one. There was a lively debate about whether I was contemptuous of the demonstrators' concerns. I had intended to depict them as ordinary decent folk, who unwittingly might encourage more sinister and dangerous forces.'

25 July 2025
Peter Schrank
The Times

'Should Keir Starmer fear the rise of Angela Rayner?' asked Sean O'Grady in the *Independent*. The *Daily Telegraph* thought that the biggest threat to Starmer came from 'his unsackable deputy, directly elected by Labour members and nakedly ambitious'. On 22 July, the 76-year-old heavy-metal singer and Black Sabbath frontman, Ozzy Osbourne, died. He had become an unlikely national treasure, but the most talked-of incident from his hell-raising days was the time, in 1982, when he bit the head off a bat thrown onstage by a fan. Osbourne had mistaken it for a toy. *Paranoid* was the band's second album and its well-known title track.

25 July 2025
Dave Brown
Independent

 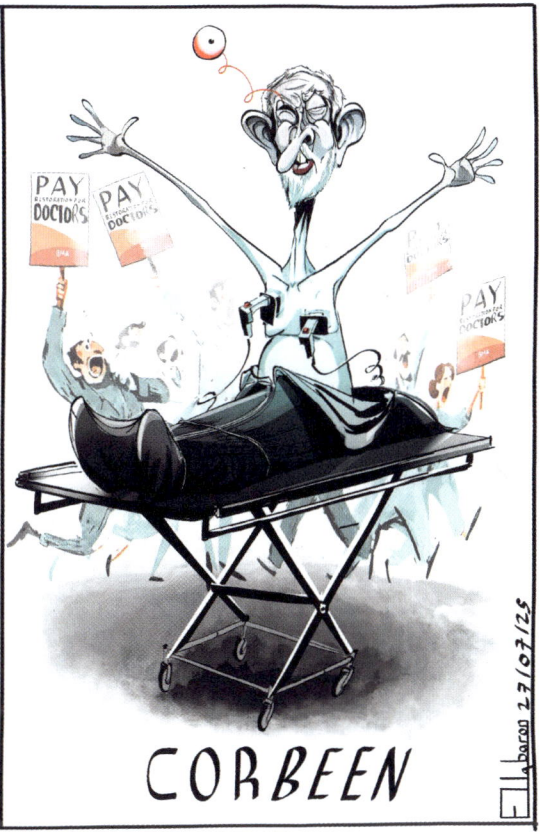

On 24 July, Jeremy Corbyn and Zarah Sultana finally launched their new political party, with Corbyn proclaiming: 'Half a million people have already signed up, but this is just the beginning!' Castigating the Labour Party as 'full of control freaks', he said that, by contrast, the new venture – temporarily branded 'Your Party' – would be 'grassroots-led' and 'fun'. The purpose, he explained, was to defend the poor and fight the rich and the corporations. The launch took place against a background of the waste-collection dispute in Birmingham and a strike by NHS resident (junior) doctors.

27 July 2025
Ella Baron
The Times

28 July 2025
Patrick Blower
Daily Telegraph

The Home Office announced the formation of a new London-based police unit, the National Internet Intelligence Investigations team. It was to be tasked with monitoring social media in order to – in the word of the policing minister – 'help local forces manage public safety threats and risks'. One motivating factor had been the protests against asylum hotels in 2024, and criticism that police forces had been unprepared; another was fear that the summer of 2025 might bring more public disorder. A former Conservative MP, Michael Fabricant, posted on X: 'When @Telegraph prints a cartoon like this, you know things are bad.'

In the last week of July, Donald Trump undertook a 'private' visit to Scotland, ostensibly to open another golf course at his Aberdeenshire property near the village of Balmedie. The course – named the Trump International Golf Links, Scotland – not only bore his family name; it was designed by his son Eric, who accompanied him on the trip. One of Trump's first acts on becoming US president in 2025 was to insist that the Gulf of Mexico be officially renamed the 'Gulf of America'. And his signature, by Sharpie pen, achieved an iconic status for the cascade of executive orders that it adorned.

30 July 2025
Steven Camley
Glasgow Herald

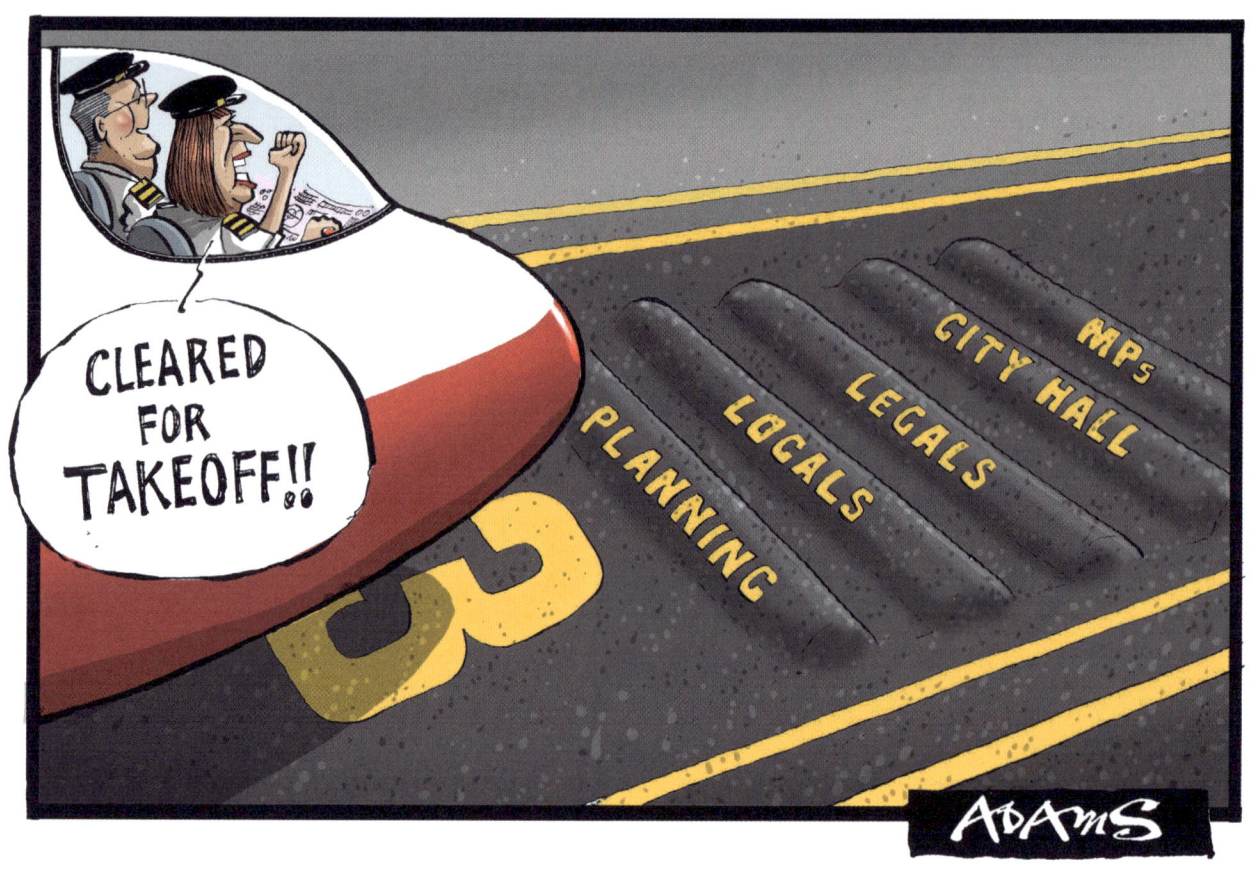

2 August 2025
Christian Adams
Daily Telegraph

With airport expansion seen as key to the government's plans to boost the economy, Sir Keir Starmer and Rachel Reeves voiced their support for the latest plan for a third runway at Heathrow, with Reeves arguing that it was 'essential' if the UK's airport capacity were to be increased. Those opposed to the notion, which has been vigorously argued over for twenty years, included communities under Heathrow's flight path, environmental campaigners, and London Mayor Sadiq Khan, who threatened to take legal action to stop the project.

While under pressure domestically over his reluctance to release files relating to the dead sex offender Jeffrey Epstein, Trump entered into a social media war of words with former Russian president Dmitry Medvedev, who had argued that, by stating that Russia faced economic sanctions if it did not agree to a ceasefire in Ukraine by 8 August, Trump was taking a 'step towards war'. Trump's response to Medvedev's 'highly provocative statements' was to order two US nuclear submarines to be moved to 'appropriate positions' in case the Russian's 'foolish and inflammatory statements are more than just that'.

4 August 2025
Nicola Jennings
Guardian

5 August 2025
Steve Bright
Sun

Amid endless challenges with the high-speed train line HS2, Home Secretary Yvette Cooper unveiled plans to introduce a different kind of 'fast-track', with a scheme to tackle the asylum backlog. Under pressure to reduce the number of asylum seekers being housed in hotels she said that this 'major overhaul' of the process would 'make quite a big reduction in the overall number in the asylum system'.

News that, since the general election, local government secretary Angela Rayner had authorised the sale of land at eight allotment sites across the country provoked the wrath of allotment devotee Jeremy Corbyn. Writing in the *Telegraph*, he claimed that 'the threat' faced by allotments from developers 'now seems to have government backing, which makes the future of these precious spaces even more perilous.'

6 August 2025
Patrick Blower
Daily Telegraph

Despite the government insisting Rachel Reeves would stick to her election pledge not to raise income tax, national insurance or VAT, senior Whitehall sources suggested that she and Sir Keir Starmer were preparing the ground for tax rises and reforms, in an effort to bridge a £41 billion spending gap. According to the cartoonist, 'Most of us send one or two idea sketches to comment page editors before drawing the final version ... On this occasion I had supplied a rough that was weak and a bit lazy. I knew this but couldn't think of anything better and time was ticking. The editor suggested I might give it another try, and the result was a stronger and clearer image.'

7 August 2025
Peter Schrank
The Times

Rushanara Ali, the parliamentary under-secretary of state for homelessness and rough sleeping, was forced to step down from her ministerial post after it emerged that, having tried and failed to sell a rental property she owned, she had then relisted it for rental at £700 a month more than she had previously charged. Since she had previously spoken out against the exploitation of private renters, she inevitably came in for accusations of 'hypocrisy and self-service' from opposition parties. The government's upcoming Renters' Rights Bill will prevent landlords who have ended a tenancy in order to sell a property from then relisting it with a higher rent until six months or more after its occupants have left.

9 August 2025
Ben Jennings
i Paper

10 August 2025
Christian Adams
Sunday Telegraph

Donald Trump announced that he would be meeting Vladimir Putin, for the first time since 2019, in Alaska on 15 August in order to discuss bringing the war in Ukraine to an end. While the US president expressed optimism about resolving the conflict, he also suggested that peace might well come at the price of Ukraine ceding territory to Russia, a proposal that Ukrainian President Volodymyr Zelensky firmly rejected. Zelensky, who was not invited to the summit, criticised peace talks that excluded Ukraine.

While in the UK for what was billed as a family holiday, American Vice-President JD Vance met Foreign Secretary David Lammy, Shadow Justice Secretary Robert Jenrick and Shadow Home Secretary Chris Philp. He also spent time with Nigel Farage at Vance's rented cottage in the Cotswolds. Since Vance was not in the UK on official business, details of this latter conversation were not – and could not be – revealed. 'Good to catch up with my old friend JD Vance this morning,' Farage said in a statement. 'Everything we discussed remains confidential.'

14 August 2025
Morten Morland
The Times

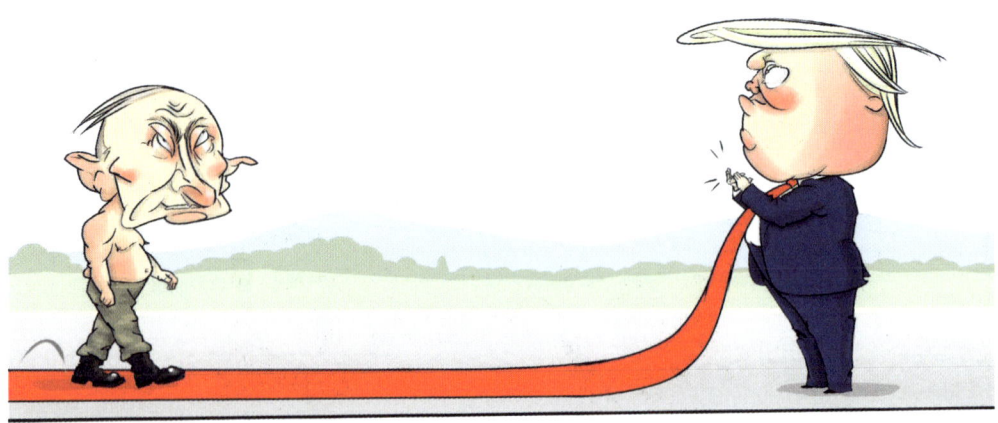

The much-heralded Trump–Putin summit in Anchorage, Alaska ended without an agreement on the war in Ukraine. The two leaders had 'had an extremely productive meeting', Trump said, but 'there's no deal until there's a deal.' In fact, the summit overall was widely seen as a win for Putin, since European hopes for a ceasefire before further negotiations were disappointed, and Putin, while being warmly received by the US president, made no concessions. Trump went on to say in an interview with Sean Hannity on Fox News: 'Now it's really up to President Zelensky to get it done and I would also say the European nations – they have to get involved a little bit.'

18 August 2025
Nicola Jennings
Guardian

On 19 August, Epping Forest District Council was successful in gaining an interim injunction to stop asylum seekers being housed at a local hotel. The Bell Hotel had become a focal point for protest when allegations emerged that an asylum seeker staying there had sexually assaulted a 14-year-old local girl. Other councils now indicated that they would take similar legal action, while such right-wing figures as Nigel Farage praised the decision: it would, he said, provide 'inspiration to others across the country'.

21 August 2025
Dave Brown
Independent

After the inconclusive Alaska summit, European leaders threatened to impose further sanctions on Russia if Vladimir Putin refused to take part in a trilateral meeting with Volodymyr Zelensky and Donald Trump. Here, Patrick Blower shows the leaders of Germany, the EU, France and Britain clustering around the US president while aiming Lilliputian insults at Russia. Trump still expressed optimism that a deal could be struck between Kyiv and Moscow, arguing that Putin was 'tired of it', but didn't elaborate on his view.

21 August 2025
Patrick Blower
Telegraph

St George's crosses and Union Jacks started appearing on lampposts and in public spaces in Weoley Castle in mid-July. They then spread across other parts of England. To some, they represented 'love, unity and patriotism'. To others, they smacked of far-right and racist sentiments. When news emerged that Essex County Council had released an email suggesting that some staff might be upset by the flags' appearance, and so require 'support', Nigel Farage accused the local authority of an 'unbelievable' over-reaction: 'some [flags are] in places they ought not to be,' he said. 'But I found this whole thing rather uplifting.' The council later stated that the offending email had not received official sanction, and that it supported people's right to 'fly the St George's cross flag with pride'.

24 August 2025
Seamus Jennings
Observer

28 August 2025
Dave Brown
Independent

On 26 August, Nigel Farage launched Reform's immigration plan, dubbed Operation Restoring Justice, suggesting a Reform government would be prepared to deport 600,000 migrants over five years. In response, Lord Hanson, a Home Office minister, said Farage was 'producing policies which I'm afraid are on the back of a fag packet' and which were 'not really deliverable in terms of what is a very complex and challenging issue.'

Two children were killed and more than a dozen people injured in Minneapolis when a gunman opened fire on pupils praying at the Church of the Annunciation, which houses the Annunciation Catholic school. FBI Director Kash Patel described the attack as 'an act of domestic terrorism motivated by a hate-filled ideology' and said the perpetrator 'left multiple anti-Catholic, anti-religious references'. The tragedy inevitably reignited the US's long-running debate about gun control, not least when it emerged that the shooter had acquired his weapon legally.

29 August 2025
Ben Jennings
Guardian

When it emerged that Angela Rayner had paid £40,000 less in stamp duty on the purchase of a flat in Hove than she would have if she had registered it as a second home, the Tories immediately called for an investigation into her tax affairs, arguing that her actions constituted 'inappropriate tax avoidance for a minister subject to higher standards of conduct'. There was no evidence that Rayner had broken any rules: while her 'primary residence' (for council tax purposes) is in her Ashton-under-Lyne constituency, following her divorce she no longer actually owns a stake in the property. In the autumn 2024 Budget, the government had increased the rate of stamp duty paid on the purchase of second homes from 3 per cent to 5 per cent.

31 August 2025
Christian Adams
Sunday Telegraph